Inner
Chatter
Matters

52 ESSAYS TO TRANSFORM
YOUR SELF-TALK

LISA PURK

Inner Chatter Matters
by Lisa Purk
Copyright ©2022 Lisa Purk

ISBN 978-1-63360-200-7

Cover design by Karen Captline, Better Be Creative, www.betterbecreative.com

                    For Worldwide Distribution   Printed in the U.S.A.

Urban Press
P.O. Box 8881
Pittsburgh, PA 15221-0881
412.646.2780
www.urbanpress.us

DEDICATION

For Mom—
you taught me to say "hi" first . . .
and so much more.

I dedicate this to you, in gratitude for a lifetime of
love, support, and encouragement.

I miss you every day.

Contents

FOREWORD

In the early days of Lisa's coaching practice, she hired me to help her learn how to effectively grow her practice. As her referral/business coach, it was easy to see Lisa's deep passion for learning, growing, and becoming a better person. She quickly became one of my favorite clients because I could always count on her to follow through with her assignments, prepare thoughtfully for our calls, and internalize and apply what she was learning not only to improve herself but also to attain her goals. Lisa understands the value of coaching and demonstrated that by her willingness to invest in herself not once, but multiple times, to achieve her success.

Lisa exhibits this same level of engagement with each of her clients. She brings her heart, soul, spirit, and faith into her work. Lisa's life experiences and years of serving young children and families as a speech language pathologist have framed her compassion and empathy, giving her a deep love for connecting with people in meaningful and fulfilling ways. I am continually impressed with Lisa's coaching intuition which helps her to authentically understand the needs of others. Her ability to equally communicate her message with honest conviction in the written word naturally moved her towards writing this book. Coaching others to overcome their fears and negative self-doubt while raising their confidence is exactly what Lisa was born to do.

Through years of supporting Lisa's growth and business development, we have become good friends. I have helped her to overcome some of her own underlying fears and self-doubts as a business owner only to watch her excel as a competent, confident life coach and now author. I know the impact she has had on the many lives she has touched and see the opportunity to extend her reach through the pages of this book. It gives me great pride to see Lisa attain this life goal of completing her first book. As a *Wall Street Journal* best-selling author, I understand everything that goes into the book-writing process and the emotional roller coaster we put ourselves through to get to this point.

Yes, there are many self-help books out there. Why this one? Lisa communicates with integrity and from the moment you start to read this book, you'll feel yourself relax knowing that you're safe and have finally found someone who truly understands you. You'll appreciate her truth and willingness to be vulnerable. The realism in her essays will touch your soul, compelling you to act and move your life closer to the dreams you envision.

I encourage you to take a deep breath and give yourself the gift waiting for you within these pages. Embrace the opportunity to reflect on your life as it is now and how it could become with Lisa's guidance. Allow Lisa to "Purk Up Your Life" as she's done for so many others just like you!

Michelle R. Donovan
- Referral/Business Coach
- Owner of Productivity Uncorked, LLC
- *Wall Street Journal* Best-Selling Author of *The 29% Solution*
- Amazon Best-Selling Author of *A Woman's Way: Empowering Female Financial Advisors to Authentically Lead and Flourish in a Man's World*

ACKNOWLEDGEMENTS

I owe a world of gratitude to so many people who have helped shape the person I am today and supported me in having the courage to publish this book.

My husband, Rick: Words fail me. Your love, your belief in me, and your gentle, but constant support have been undying. You are the love of my life. Thank you for coming back.

Dr. John Stanko: For your direction, editing, and fine-tuning my words in the places it was needed. Most of all, for your patience, encouragement, and words of wisdom when I didn't think I had the courage to finish.

Regina Russo: For the laughter, the tears, and the talks that turned lunches into dinners. You are my friend. Forever.

Karen Captline: What would I do without your friendship and your graphic design genius? Thank you is not nearly enough. You make my world a much better place, all because of ARC notebooks.

Michelle Donovan and Patty Kreamer: For believing in me even when I was still on a journey to believe in myself. Your encouragement, mentoring, and friendship have been a blessing in my life.

My loyal Friday blog readers: I took time off when Mom died and when I returned, with fear of seeing a massive number of unsubscribes, you emailed me with warm messages that said, "We're glad you're back; we missed you."

My coaching clients: You tell me that you learn from me.

But it is I who has learned so much more from you. Thank you for trusting me to be the help you were seeking.

And so many others without whom my life wouldn't be as meaningful. I wouldn't be in business because I would have quit and this book would still just be pages in my mind: Chris Cosky, Coralee Gionta, Sue Kantz, and Cindy Winslow.

To all of you, and so many more, my heartfelt gratitude that reaches beyond words.

INTRODUCTION

When I was a young girl, I was excruciatingly shy. I would often complain to Mom that someone hadn't said 'hi' to me or included me in a game.

My mom would, without fail, ask me, "Did you say 'hi' first?"

Equally without fail I would answer, "Well, no."

Because in my young mind, if someone didn't say 'hi' or include me in a game, they clearly didn't like me. *So, why would I say 'hi' first?* I would think to myself.

These thoughts of not being liked and others not wanting to include me went on through grade school, high school, and college. Although I would like to say it ended then, it continued into my early adult years.

When I was in my 30s, (ahem, late 30s), a friend asked me, "Where does that come from? I don't get it; why don't you think people like you?" She went on to say, "You're loving, kind, caring, and fun to be around."

"Why don't you think people like you?" she repeated.

My answer was, "I don't know; it's just there."

In retrospect, I realize my internal belief was that I had pre-programmed thoughts given to me at birth, and these were mine with which to navigate life. Someone else, like my friend, was given different, more confident thoughts.

It was with these thoughts of being unworthy, undeserving, and tolerated but not loved that I lived my life. I knew I wanted more for my life and my relationships, but thoughts of "those things aren't meant for me; maybe someone else, but not for me" were my constant companions.

Until something happened when I was in my 40s.

I attended a seminar which presented a strong personal development component. The leader described inner thoughts we have and told us how, if we're not careful, those thoughts will hold us back from the things we want in life. He described thoughts of "not being good enough" (or "smart enough" or "old enough" or "young enough"). Maybe you have some of these same thoughts.

He talked about thoughts of no one loving, or even liking, us. (Uh oh, now he was getting personal! How did he know?)

That day was the first time I heard the phrase, *Itty Bitty Shitty Committee.*

"Oh, I like that one," I chuckled.

I learned two things that day. First, I wasn't the only one who had negative and defeating inner chatter that kept me in a place that I didn't want to be.

And second, I had a choice. Just as I was spending my life thinking negatively about myself, I could just as easily be thinking positive, encouraging, and kind thoughts about who I am and the value I have to offer.

I went on a journey to learn how to release the defeating inner chatter I was holding on to and replace it with words and thoughts that would propel me forward into the life and relationships I so desperately desired. In doing so, my life completely changed.

The stories I share with you in this book are from my life. They range from simple, everyday scenarios like food choices and smiles from strangers to difficult, emotional times like witnessing my parents grow old. There are happy stories such as enjoying a bike ride or walking my mom's energetic beagle, but there are sadder stories here, too. However, all of the stories have one thing in common.

They all remind me, "I have a choice in how I speak to myself." I get to choose what perspectives I live by. And you do, too.

This book is divided into 52 essays. You can read them in any order. It is not necessary to start with the first and read through to the last, although that works just as well as reading them randomly. Sometimes I open a book and read that page and find it's just what I need for that day. This is another way to consume each of the essays I share here. Whatever you choose, make it your own.

I encourage you to take time with each one, freely highlighting and making notes. Reflect and let them percolate in your mind. Use a journal to dig deeper into your own thoughts and feelings. Answer the questions to guide you in your time of reflection. Take what you learned into your day and look for ways each lesson applies to your own life.

Keep your heart and mind open to allow each story to inspire you to create the life you desire. Let them serve as a reminder that today, and every day, you have a choice. A choice that always begins with your self-talk.

When you change your inner chatter, you change your life.

It really does matter.

Lisa Purk
Beaver Falls, PA
November 2022

A BEAGLE NAMED PHIL

"The secret of change is to focus all of your energy not on
fighting the old, but on building the new."
~ Socrates

As Mom continued to heal from a fractured pelvis, my husband and I helped her in as many ways as we could. One of those ways was taking care of her dog, Phil—easy-going, affectionate, and all beagle.

Phil enjoys going for walks. Now mind you, walks are not his number one favorite thing. Number one is being scratched. Behind the ears, back, or belly, it doesn't matter: "Just *please* scratch me," he begs with his beagle eyes. His number two favorite thing is eating, preferably his bacon treats. Then in third place and always welcome is a walk, the approval evidenced by his enthusiastic response when he sees his harness and leash. I forgot to mention his love for digging a hole to escape under the fence and go for a hunt in the woods. But for now, let's stick with the walk.

Here's the thing about Phil on a walk. He can barely stand still as I put his harness on him as he bounces side to side. Then, with a surge of beagle energy, he bursts through the gate. As we cross the road and start down the block, he is all butt-wiggle. He looks up at me with eyes of pure joy about this adventure we're on. And this all lasts, oh, maybe another minute before he stops, sits down, and looks up as if to say, "I'm done. Can we go home now? I can't take another step." And this is how he is for the remainder of our walk—all that initial enthusiasm expended in the first minute.

Phil always made me smile and I hope his story makes you smile, too. But there's also something to learn from him. Think about a time you have started out of the gate with great enthusiasm for:

- Writing a book
- Planting a garden
- Following a nutrition and exercise plan
- Staying organized
- Being on time
- Rising earlier in the morning
- Insert yours here _____

Are you like Phil? Do you start with great energy and enthusiasm only to burn out within a few days, maybe a week? Do you follow this same pattern — every single time? One reason people, perhaps even you, fail to stick to their plans is they don't actually have a plan.

All changes in life, even the ones you choose for yourself, are going to impact your routines, your relationships, and the boundaries of your comfort zone. You must consider how you will manage these three areas. You must be willing to adapt along the way as more changes arise. And you must be willing to navigate your way through the discomfort until it isn't uncomfortable any longer and has, in fact, become beautifully comfortable.

And you wonder why you ever sat down and said, "I'm done now."

CHECK IN WITH YOUR INNER CHATTER

1. Of all the things you have been putting off, which one do you want to get started on right away?
2. Before you get started on something new, you may need to eliminate something old to create time and energy for the new. What is it?
3. What changes in your work or personal habits do you need to make that will undergird the new thing(s) you want to do?

A FENDER BENDER BENDS MY THINKING

"The smallest deed is better than the greatest intention." ~ John Burroughs

I recall a time Mom experienced what we commonly term a "fender bender." There was minor damage to the two vehicles, but no injuries. As Mom turned right out of a parking lot, she trusted the turn signal of the oncoming car. His turn signal indicated, "I'm turning here" but he didn't. The police report stated the accident was Mom's fault.

"But he had on his turn signal," a fact the other driver did not dispute. As the policeman explained, however, "A turn signal is an *indication* that a driver *might* make a turn, but it's not a certainty or a legal obligation."

This reminds me of times I've put something on my "to-do" list, only to look at it later, shake my head, and think, *Said I would but never did.* I confess that my intent probably wasn't wholehearted. Oftentimes, though, I could say I had good intentions. The thing I didn't have was follow through.

I turned on my turn signal but never turned. As Mom's accident was filed as her fault, my lack of follow through is mine.

After that experience, Mom always chose to wait and be certain a vehicle was turning before pulling in front of it. In other words, she changed her actions.

I can say the same for myself. When I notice myself making lists of what I want to accomplish, I must accompany that with a plan. I always include:

- Who? In addition to myself, I identify who else is involved or impacted by this task.
- What? I take time to identify all the steps required from start to finish.
- When? I look at my calendar and plan when I will complete each step.

And most important of all, I ask myself: *What mindset do I need to complete this project. Are there fears I need to manage?* I know I won't take any of the three steps above if I let fear be in charge.

Turn signal or not, Mom learned to wait.

I learned to expect more of myself.

CHECK IN WITH YOUR INNER CHATTER

1. What is something you find yourself repeatedly putting on your to-do list?

2. How would you identify the who, what, and when?

3. Are there fears associated with completing these tasks? What can you do to help yourself manage those fears?

WHAT'S BROCCOLI GOT TO DO WITH IT?

"You can act your way into feeling long before you can feel your way into action." ~ Unknown

It was morning and time to prepare breakfast.

I had planned eggs, bacon, an English muffin, and some type of sautéed greens. I add the greens to breakfast so I get more of their nutrition each day. I have also learned that sautéed greens are quite good with eggs, so I don't usually mind—except some mornings are different. Like this one.

I was just getting past several days of being sick, the on-the-couch-not-going-anywhere kind of sick. I didn't have much appetite and throughout those days I kept saying, "I'm just not hungry; nothing sounds good."

And so, with slowly returning levels of energy and appetite, I was happy to be hungry. The above breakfast sounded good except for the greens. I just didn't want them. This all reminded me of a story a client told of listening to a speaker tout the benefits of broccoli.

He wholeheartedly believed in eating certain amounts of broccoli daily. This gentleman went on to say that he often has the opportunity to share this information with others. But in doing so, he often hears, "But I don't like broccoli" to which he responds, "What does liking it have to do with anything?"

To him, the important factor was the health benefits so, therefore, you eat it whether you like the taste and texture or not. But broccoli and the benefits or how much of it to eat are not my point. In fact, neither is eating greens for breakfast or any other encouragement to eat healthy (although I believe it's a great idea).

I did, however, find the question, "What does 'like it' have to do with anything?" an interesting one. It is one that has often stirred in my head just as it did on this "I've been sick for a week" morning.

Did I have to "feel like" eating the greens in order to choose to include them? Not only is that an interesting one to me, but I also believe the value of this question goes beyond food choices.

There are many things in life we may not "feel like doing" or we may not "like" and yet we know our lives will be better for doing them (or in some cases not doing them). The examples are endless so place your own "in my best interest" items into this story.

There will be days it's easy to stick to the plans you've set for yourself. But there will be those other days that no matter what, you just "don't feel like it." You may use words like, "That's just hard for me; It's not really 'me' to do that; I wish I could; or maybe tomorrow." But more than the easy days, these harder days, the ones that take discipline and determination, are the ones that make a difference in the achievements you see in your life.

With some adaption to my original plans, I ate the greens. I didn't sauté them; I ate raw spinach and tomatoes (read as "still fatigued; less cooking; less pans to wash") instead. It's still a good choice with eggs. It's still adding the greens.

This time, I didn't eat them by desire.

I did it by choice.

CHECK IN WITH YOUR INNER CHATTER

1. What words do you use when you notice yourself in resistance? Are they encouraging and helping you to make progress? Or are they negative and holding you back?

2. What difference does it make to your life when you act in spite of your resistance?

3. What thoughts help you to be in action rather than resistance?

BUT I'M TOO OLD FOR THAT

"Two roads diverged in a wood and I—I took
the one less traveled by, and that has made all
the difference." ~ Robert Frost

Our society has common notions about age that are frequently repeated in everyday conversations. Think about how often you have been told about the achy muscles and joints you are certain to have after you turn 40. And how many times have you heard "Your body just falls apart after 50"? Or you set out to try something new and someone says, "Oh, you can't do *that* at *your* age."

Spoken with a laugh, these comments also carry a tone that says, "It's true and there's nothing you can do about it."

The thing you don't often hear is "You have another option."

I was born in 1960 so you can do the math. Or, to make it easy, at the time of this writing, I'm 60. So, there's no shortage of times I've heard these exact messages. But I want to choose something different; I want to "take the road less traveled."

I'm not blind to the fact that some things will require extra effort because yes, age has had its impact. But I also know that I want to maintain strength, flexibility, and mobility throughout my later decades. And if these three things are going to be a reality for me, I am the one who must make it happen.

Exercise has long been an on-again, off-again endeavor for me and a few months ago, it was time to make it on-again. So, when a space opened in a 5:30 a.m. exercise class that meets four mornings a week just one mile from my home, I had no room for excuses. When I signed up for my first eight-week commitment, my goal was to simply get there and participate. Aware of others around me who were clearly stronger than I was, I stayed focused on my own journey by telling myself, "You're here; that's what matters."

It wasn't long before a felt a little stronger and worked a little harder. I was gaining the flexibility and mobility I desired, and I knew I was stronger by the improvements I noted as I completed each exercise. But I didn't think there were any visible physical results. I was okay with that because improvements were evident in other ways. But hey, who am I kidding? I knew visible results would be nice as well.

And so, it was an awesome surprise when I received a picture and text from owner and fitness instructor Chris Cosky at B Well Nation telling me, "We exercise for improved mental health. We exercise for physical good health. We exercise so our instructors can take a kick ass picture of our strong back and shoulders in a power pose! Look at you!"

I admit this text made my day. It inspired me to want to do even better. I felt stronger just seeing it—both mentally and physically. It highlighted one piece of my journey to maintaining flexibility and mobility.

But I'm not sharing these stories for me; I'm writing them for you. Therefore, I ask you to think about how often you:

- Give up—or don't even start—because you think "I'm too old for that," whether it's something physical or something else you'd like to do?

- Listen to family, friends, or society in general when they try to instill limits on what you can do?

- Think, *Oh it's too late for me* or *That's just the way life is*?

I encourage you to believe you were made for more.

Trash the notion that it's "just the way life is" or "it's as good as it gets." Resist the path that's dull, boring, and too much of the same old thing.

Instead, take the road less traveled where there's beauty and reward to be discovered.

Take the road where you find your strength.

CHECK IN WITH YOUR INNER CHATTER

1. What is something you want to do but find yourself saying, "I'm too old for that?" (Or maybe for you, it's a different "too much of, too little of, or not enough of.") What is that thing you want to do?

2. Ask yourself, "Is it true, beyond a shadow of a doubt, that I can't do this thing?"

3. Next, ask, "What if I *could* do this thing" and identify one small action step you can take toward making it happen. Focus on taking that step and the next will reveal itself, but only if you take a step forward.

BUT I WANT COCA-COLA

"Life is a matter of choices, and every choice
you make makes you." ~ John C. Maxwell

I like Coca-Cola.

I don't like the upward shift in weight in causes; the unhealthy changes in blood sugar levels; or the late-in-the-day aftertaste it leaves in my mouth.

But in the moment that it's fresh, ice cold, and fizzy? Then it's hard for me to resist.

I do resist it most of the time for the reasons I mentioned—at least the weight and blood sugar. I'm willing to deal with the aftertaste. It's best for me not to have the soda around at all. Its temptation is strong and so very real for me.

But whether it's easily available is not always up to me. Even if both my husband and I avoid having it at home, I work in a space with a shared kitchen and a refrigerator that often has soda available.

First thing in the morning it's easy to avoid; even lunchtime presents little problem. But by mid-afternoon, I start to hear it calling my name.

I've learned to say to myself, "I want it but I'm choosing not to have it."

If I say, "I don't want it," then it's a lie. Truthfully, I do want it and telling myself otherwise causes an internal tug of war between "I don't" and "I do" that usually leads to drinking it because it eases the stress of the battle.

But if I acknowledge, "Yes I want it" but follow-up with "But I'm choosing not to have it," then I am in control.

When I feel in control of the choice, I am much more likely to make the one that's best for me.

I do occasionally choose to have the soda. More frequently, I choose to have the water instead.

That also doesn't leave an aftertaste of regret.

Bonus.

CHECK IN WITH YOUR INNER CHATTER

1. What is something you often want but know it's in your best interests to choose not to have it?

2. Why is it important to you to make the new choice? What will keep you inspired to make the more beneficial choice?

3. Name three new things you can substitute in place of the old habit. For example, if it's something that helps you relax (yes, sugar has a calming effect for me), what else will create that same calming effect without the downside?

DIGGING BELOW THE SURFACE

"I went to the woods because I wished to live deliberately, to front only the essential facts of life, and see if I could not learn what it had to teach, and not, when I came to die, discover that I had not lived." ~ Henry David Thoreau

Some of my favorite times in life are those spent with friends over a cup of coffee or a meal. It's the kind of time you spend sharing what's going on in your life and talking about important things. You share what's in your heart and on your mind with a keen awareness of your vulnerability. These are times with moments of laughter and sometimes a tear or two. Then there's the moment you simultaneously look at the time and exclaim, "Really, we've been here that long!" And because it's much later than you thought, you scurry off, but you do so with a hug that says, "Thanks, this was fun" and a promise to "do this again soon."

It was in the midst of one of these conversations when a friend and I decided to dig into the question, "Why do so many people keep their relationships (of all kinds) at a surface level?" We shared a few different thoughts including that people are afraid; and once again, fear comes into the picture of our lives.

Why do we fear deeper relationships? Why are we so drawn to finding and maintaining relationships that rarely, if ever, go beyond the surface—ones that do not bring happiness, fulfillment, and closeness? One answer to this question is the surface is safe: there's much less risk at the surface. One reason there is less risk is in how much we stand to lose.

In order to discover deeper, more meaningful relationships with others, we must also risk losing them. We can't find them if we aren't willing to lose them. That's not to say we *will* lose them, but we must be willing to do so because that's the chance we take. And we all know that the loss of a deep, meaningful, and fulfilling relationship hurts.

The alternative is to never take the chance, but by doing so, we've already lost something. We live with the discomfort of unfulfilling relationships with others because it's easier than risking the discomfort of loss.

As I drove away from this particular time of good coffee, good food, and even better conversation and friendship, I asked myself the question, "In what other situations do people stay at the surface?"

And now I ask you, where else are you staying at the surface? What area of your life do you want to commit to wander out of your comfort zone and do what it takes to get what you want?

Yes, if you go deeper, you *might* lose.

If you stay at the surface, you already have.

CHECK IN WITH YOUR INNER CHATTER

1. What area of your life occupied your thoughts as you read this story?

2. In what ways would your life be different if you made a choice to take the risk and go deeper to create the results you truly desire?

3. Is today the day you'll get rid of your safety net and go after the life and relationships you want?

ARE YOU DEVOTED?

"Finally, brothers, whatever is true, whatever is
honorable, whatever is just, whatever is pure,
whatever is lovely, whatever is commendable,
if there is any excellence, if there is anything
worthy of praise, think about these things."
~ Philippians 4:8

Anyone who knows me well, or even casually for
that matter, knows how much my morning time means to
me. It is quiet time spent with God, a time when I am intentional about growing my relationship with Him. It is a time
I dig deeper to learn more about myself through journaling.
My morning routine is a habit too valuable to ever abandon.

It was on one such morning that the words *devotion* and *meditation* stirred in my mind. I use these words
often, especially meditation, as in "I plan to read my daily
meditation."

But do I use them with due reverence to their meaning? Or is it without?

It is easy to read a morning devotion and think,
"Wow, that was powerful" and then quickly move on with
my day. Perhaps you have done this as well.

But am I truly devoted when I do this?

I believe daily *devotions* and *meditations* are given
those labels for a reason. They are meant for us to reflect
and discover their deeper meaning for our lives. They are
written to call us to a fuller, more complete life. Sometimes
they confirm, other times they convict. Always, when we
approach them with a devoted and meditative mentality,
they change us.

To engage in devotion and reflective meditation

around something, we must take the time to do so. We must be willing to commit our time and energy to it. Then, we must be willing to take what has been learned and carry it into our daily words, attitudes, and actions.

Otherwise, *devotion* and *meditation* are just two more words casually used in our vocabulary.

In my life, if I want my morning time to be life changing, I must dig beneath the surface.

I must be devoted.

CHECK IN WITH YOUR INNER CHATTER

1. What meaning do the words *devotion* and *meditation* have for you?

2. What is something you rush through but know you would benefit from engaging it with more devotion and care?

3. What new action steps can help you do this?

FIGHTING TO EXCEL

"Whatever you do today, do it with the
confidence of a four-year-old in a Batman
t-shirt." ~ Unknown

I long ago declared that I hate Excel. I had no desire to learn it and worked around it any way I could. I also
didn't need to learn it.

Until I did—need to learn it that is.

In one of my roles in life, I mentored business owners. I also submitted monthly reports. When I started to
handle these, the current contract year was already set-
up for me in Excel. All I had to do was enter data. Simple
enough.

But then the new contract year loomed ahead of me.

I was scared and anxious. I also didn't have any way
to work around using it.

I dug into on-line training courses. Boring in places
(yes, I know how to save a file) but (I can't believe I'm saying
this) also fun and truthfully, not all that hard.

But then came the true test. I had to convert the
spreadsheet for the past year and prepare new ones for the
coming year. This required removing last year's data while
maintaining formulas for the coming year.

For all the times I reminded myself, "You have last
year's saved on your computer *and* on a jump drive" I was
nervous. I paced. I refreshed my coffee. I made an extra
bathroom run . . . or two. I talked to my husband. And I
paced some more.

In other words, I procrastinated. Because of anxiety
that I would totally screw up the reports, I put off what was
needed.

When we put off and procrastinate because we feel anxious, it can be because we are fearful that we don't have the knowledge or skill to complete the task.

My solution was to first put myself in a quiet location. I even joked with my husband, (after interrupting his work, of course), "You may not be allowed to talk to me." Then I took my time and thought through each step before I took it. I continued to remind myself that I had the old report saved if I needed to start over, and that I did indeed have the skill needed to conquer this task.

I completed the new report templates and readied them for the new contract year, and I didn't even have to start over—not even once.

When you're feeling anxious and find yourself procrastinating, ask yourself, "Do I have the skill to do this?" If a new skill is needed, then seek to learn it. If you already have the skill, then take the first step as you remind yourself that you do have the intelligence and talent to complete the task.

You might even find you excel.

CHECK IN WITH YOUR INNER CHATTER

1. What have you been putting off out of anxiety that you don't have the skill to do it? Do you need to learn a new skill or simply boost your confidence that you already have the skill?

2. Taking it a step further, what is something you really *want* to do but fear you're not smart enough, talented enough, or disciplined enough? (Or another "not enough" scenario that plays out in your mind)

3. What experience left you thinking you can't? Recognize that the experience you had in the past, and this new desire you have now, are two different things. Who says you can't?

EMBRACING THE Q

"There are always two choices, two paths to
take. One is easy. And its only reward is that it's
easy." ~ Unknown

It was the Scrabble tournament of the century. Well,
I admit that is quite an exaggeration, but it was *our* tournament. That alone made it special.

But let me back up to a few weeks earlier.

The Christmas season had arrived with its annual
display of lights and calendars booked with shopping, decorating, and holiday parties. Our house was decorated, the
cookies were baked, and we hosted a party for a few close
friends. By the time December 24 arrived, we had also delivered pumpkin bread to our neighbors and stocked our
cupboards with our favorite foods.

But even so, our plans that year mostly included just
the two of us, my husband and I, and a welcome eleven days
off from work. This was welcome because we were in much
need of rest; not the kind that comes from sleep but rather
the kind that allows one's brain to take a break from typical
daily tasks.

Looking forward to this time off, we spent December
making a list of possible activities we agreed would be fun to
do during our time off. Nowhere on that list was, "Scrabble
tournament." The phrase, "play games," wasn't even there.

So, I'm not quite certain how Scrabble came into
play, but it did—as did a best-of-seven tournament. I confess that I came up with the idea when I lost the first game.

At about game three or four, the ever-so-common
grumbling of picking a Q, a Z or even an X from the box
could be heard. Chin dropping, deep sigh complaining like,

"Oh, I didn't seriously just draw that letter, did I?" A selection of a Q was also followed by a quick calculation of whether I had a U, if there was one available on the board, or whether there were even any left to draw from the remaining letters. In case you didn't know, there are four U's available in Scrabble.

You may also like to know that Qi is a valid Scrabble word—no "u" required.

But, moving on.

As we set up for our next game, Rick asked a contemplative question: "Why do we grumble about picking a Q or a Z?". Continuing the thought, he offered, "They're the high point letters and help us win the game. We want to win, so why complain?"

I high-fived him for that shift in perspective. "You're so right" I affirmed as I made a mental note to write it in my collection of book topics.

If I apply it to life beyond Scrabble, I ask, "Why do we complain about the opportunity to do the very thing that helps us win?"

We don't like those letters because they're hard to use. We're not confident that we will figure out a word and have a board location for them. We must think and work our brains. And we worry we won't be able to use them and will lose points. Although the occasional "quit," "query" or "zero" happens along easily, most often we must work hard to use our Q's and Z's.

But when we do, we score high points like the time I put "quiz" on a triple word for 64 points.

How often do you grumble about doing that which will help you achieve something you want for yourself? for your business? for your life?

For example, do you

- complain about eating a healthy food when energy or weight loss is your goal?

- grumble about getting up earlier when spending time in quiet reading, prayer, and journaling are what you desire to do?

- fuss about attending an evening networking event when taking your business to the next level is your intention?

- go on about the shoes you passed up because you are committed to getting your finances in order?

As you consider the amazing opportunities available to you, recognize that your boldest actions, biggest wins, and greatest successes will come by doing things that challenge you.

Your success will come when you embrace the Q.

CHECK IN WITH YOUR INNER CHATTER

1. What is the "Q" in your life? What is something you want but know it will be a challenge for you to accomplish it?

2. What level of confidence do you have that you can indeed "win" at achieving it? Would developing your confidence be of value in helping you meet the challenge?

3. How will your life be different when you conquer the challenge rather than give in to excuses?

I'M STUCK ON STICKERS

"Dare to be different and distinct and totally you. Anything else would just be a waste of the incredible person you were designed to be and, quite frankly, an insult to God." ~ Ann Vertel

I really love stickers.

When I was a young girl, nothing was more exciting at school than earning a gold star for my forehead or a larger star of any color at the top of a worksheet I had completed well.

At an early morning exercise class I attend, they offer stickers for our personal attendance sheet. It's a great way for me to track how often I go to class and if I'm meeting my goals—a serious and functional reason for stickers. But honestly, that's just my excuse for using them.

The real reason is the quiet sense of joy I get making my choice of what sticker to use after each class.

Different reasons guide my choosing. Some days, it reflects the effort it took for me to get to class; other days it's an accomplishment in class; and sometimes I pick the rainbow because rainbows remind me of heaven and of Mom and Dad. There's always a different reason for the one I pick. The constant is the joy each one brings.

It took me a while to accept this fact. I thought I was "too old" for stickers; those were for kids. "What value do those really bring you?" I would hear myself ask. I hid the fact that I loved them and didn't share the quiet joy they gave me. I harbored thoughts like *That would be embarrassing* or *people will ridicule me behind my back*.

In time, I began to fully embrace stickers. I have purchased a stack of them. I have stars, smiley faces, feathers, and flowers—and I have rainbows. And I use them. I put them in my journal to announce the end of an entry or near a new revelation I've had about myself or my life. I even put them in books I'm reading when something stands out to me. "Look here; this is important" they tell me.

I now tell people that I love stickers. I have been gifted stickers and they remind me of someone special when I use them.

And so, the question, "What value do stickers bring?"

For me, they have high value.

They bring me joy. I have fun when I use them. I anticipate opportunities and they keep me engaged in writing, reading, and learning. They are a simple way for me to acknowledge accomplishments. And they connect me with others in fun ways when I'm willing to be vulnerable and admit the joy they bring.

Stickers help me let go of unreasonable and unwarranted restrictions. "Who said they're only for kids? Who said I'm too old to enjoy them? Who said they have no real value for my life?"

Maybe their most important value came the day I said, "I enjoy them."

And that's reason enough for me.

CHECK IN WITH YOUR INNER CHATTER

1. What are simple things or activities that bring you joy during your days? Some ideas include lighting a candle, burning essential oils, or listening to soothing music.

2. Are you frequently allowing yourself to experience these simple joys? Why or why not?

3. Do you have worry or self-doubt that prevents you from enjoying them? What new thoughts can you focus on to replace your self-sabotaging inner chatter?

IT REALLY IS THAT EASY

"Believe you can and you're halfway there."
~ Theodore Roosevelt

My day started at 4:45 a.m. That's usually a good thing for me as I am most definitely a "morning person." But it also means that by a certain time in the evening (and we're not talking late evening) my brain shuts down. "That is all," it tells me.

So, after a busy day, including both physically as well as emotionally fatiguing activities, my husband and I were headed home. My mind soothed itself with two images: comfortable clothes (i.e., pajamas) and laying my head on my pillow. "Ahhh, yes," just the thought of it.

Yep, "ahhh" right up until the moment my mind interrupted with, "Excuse me, but what about those emails you need to send tonight? People are waiting for your information."

"Oh, dang," (I may or may not be substituting a word for what actually came out of my mouth) I said as my chin dropped to my chest. "What's up" my husband asked. I explained.

And then I remembered watching a short video clip from Kerwin Rae that encouraged using the words, "It's simple; it's easy; it's fun." I started to repeat them to myself. "It's simple, it's easy, it's fun."

Did it work? Like a lucky charm.

My body relaxed and my mind alerted me as to what was needed. Arriving home, I started the computer and as it booted up, I got into those comfortable clothes. I prepped what was needed and got it sent off, even adding a bonus activity with the energy I supplied myself with that simple phrase, "It's simple, it's easy, it's fun."

I could have grumbled and been miserable as I completed what was needed. (Yes, that temptation lurked). But I was going to do it either way so why not find a way to be positive and relaxed in the process?

The next time your chin is hitting your chest, and you're sighing and uttering stressful words, choose instead to pick your head up, relax your shoulders, and choose some empowering words. (Hint: Repeat those words more than once; repeat them until you begin to feel your energy shift.)

Like me, you're going to do this thing anyway.

Why be miserable when you can choose simple, easy, and fun instead?

CHECK IN WITH YOUR INNER CHATTER

1. What is your usual response when you have a task to complete but you're fatigued and stressed?
2. Do you believe you can shift your response through the words you choose?
3. What cues can you use to remind yourself to shift your response?

A RUNNER LAPPED ME

"There is nothing noble in being superior to
your fellow man; true nobility is being superior
to your former self." ~ Ernest Hemingway

Outdoors is my favorite place to spend time. I love the beach, but I enjoy time in the mountains as well. A day sitting by a lake or biking along a wooded trail easily makes my "favorite way to spend a day" list. But I can't do these every day. And so, I often choose to spend time at a local park where I can trek into the woods for a longer, thoroughly rejuvenating hike or a short jaunt around the walking trail.

One morning, when I had only a brief amount of time, I decided to spend that time on the one-mile loop. Shortly into my walk, a runner passed me. This wasn't too surprising since I was walking, and he was jogging. But a little while later, he passed me again, having jogged that loop fast enough to catch and run by me a second time. I chuckled to myself as I thought, *Ha! That dude just lapped me.*

I wasn't comparing myself to him, so I didn't become upset that I "wasn't doing enough" or "I should be jogging." For me, the important thing was, "I'm out here." The easy path would have been to stay home, and I could have listed quite a few reasons to do so. But what was in my best interests, for a list of even more valuable reasons was to go for a morning walk. I was out there.

Then a short time later, I passed two women who were walking slower than I for whatever reason. Maybe they chose a leisurely walk that day or possibly something in their physical condition made it difficult to walk any faster. I didn't know nor did it matter to me. The thing I did know was they were there spending time together and were walking. They were out there.

There is no benefit when you compare yourself to others. Sure, I was slower than the runner; I was faster than the two women. But what point would there be in focusing on that? The more important point then and in life is whether I was participating, not whether I was doing better than the other person. The value comes in doing better than I did yesterday.

Whether it's getting exercise, eating healthier, starting your day earlier, energizing your marriage, building a business, or whatever you want to improve in some way, the question is, "Are you in the game?" Or are your excuses winning?

Are you out there?

CHECK IN WITH YOUR INNER CHATTER

1. What is something in your life you are resisting because you're mentally comparing yourself to what others are doing (or you think they're doing)?

2. What is one thing you can do today that is more than you did yesterday?

3. How do you feel participating rather than surrendering to your excuses?

A SHIFT IN PERSPECTIVE

"Progress is impossible without change, and
those who cannot change their minds cannot
change anything." ~ George Bernard Shaw

I had a shoulder issue that was causing a significant
amount of pain and greatly reduced my range of motion.

The problem started quite a while before I sought
help, so how about we won't count how long I ignored it?
When I finally decided to address it, I first went to see my
physician—twice. Then I started with one chiropractor (he
was good, but 45 minutes away from home) and physical
therapy.

As I was trying to figure out what to do next, I met
another chiropractor whose office was five minutes from
home, which was much more conducive to regular visits.
I listened intently as he described the symptoms of "fro-
zen shoulder." As he did, I mentally said, "Check, check,
check. Yep, I've got them all." Needless to say, I made an
appointment.

One day, as I was getting ready to go to my next appointment, I anticipated his asking, "How is your shoulder
doing?" I started to plan how I was going to tell him, "Well,
I still can't . . ."

Then I thought, "But wait, I can . . ." and I was able
to name at least ten things I could do that I hadn't been able
to do just a week earlier. It was true that internal rotation
(i.e., reaching behind my back to hook a certain female undergarment) was still not possible. I was also still waking up
with pain at night. But I could reach over and behind my

head, grab something from a higher shelf, take a shirt off over my head, and put my coat on without help—to name a few. Side planks were now in my repertoire of possibility again. This represented huge progress.

And so, it was time to ask myself the question, "Am I going to focus on what I can't yet do or focus on all the progress I have made?"

I think it is easy and a common habit for many people to focus on what hasn't yet been accomplished. This can create a feeling of disappointment and a sense of "I'll never get there." It definitely doesn't inspire one to move forward. But when we're willing to first highlight the progress, we will feel much more grounded, confident, and ready to take action toward that which has so far remained elusive.

When you find yourself talking about all you haven't yet accomplished, stop, and acknowledge what has. Then take your next step.

In a short period of time, I was able to sleep pain-free, could stretch further, hold the side plank for longer, and lift a heavier weight to strengthen the affected muscles. I didn't ignore what I still wanted to accomplish, but I cultivated a willingness to look at the progress I had made. This helped me maintain my momentum and inspired me to continue working toward my goals. It took a little longer for the pain-free hooking of the undergarment, but eventually, I got there too.

Now that was an accomplishment.

CHECK IN WITH YOUR INNER CHATTER

1.   What is something you have started but haven't reached your ultimate goal?

2.   Are you focused on what you haven't yet accomplished or the progress you've made?

3.   In what ways can you be more focused on accomplishments?

MANAGING "YEA BUT" RESPONSES

"Every decision you make—every decision—
is not a decision about what to do. It is a
decision about who you are. When you see
this, when you understand this, everything
changes. You begin to see life in a new way. All
events, occurrences, and situations turn into
opportunities to do what you came here to do."
~ Neale Donald Walsch

My intention is to eat more vegetables every day. I have reasons beyond the "vegetables are good for you" chorus we often hear. But in full disclosure, vegetables are not my favorite thing to include in my food choices. They're not spelled b-r-e-a-d . . . enough said.

So simple strategies are critical and the only way I'll make this happen. First, I've discovered that I need to add them to the things I already eat and enjoy. Chopped broccoli in macaroni salad or chopped green pepper in a basil pesto quinoa are two of my recent creations. The macaroni salad looked so good to my husband that he added some to his, too. That was a bonus.

One morning not long ago I was figuring out a quick, "I only have a few minutes" breakfast for myself. As I prepared a favorite of sprouted grain toast with sliced hard-boiled egg, I thought, "Stacking some fresh spinach on here would taste good and add some desired veggies."

"Yea but," my mind quickly warned, "you don't have any spinach."

I could have stopped there. In the past I would have.

Another excuse not to eat the veggies. More b-r-e-a-d for me, please.

On this morning though, I didn't stop at "yea but." Instead, I offered to no one but myself, "You do have green pepper."

So, I created an open-faced sandwich of toast layered with sliced green pepper and hard-boiled egg, plus a spread of hot pepper mustard to add a spark of extra flavor. It was delicious and actually better with the added green pepper.

If I had stopped at the first "yea but" I would have been stuck in old patterns that seemed like the perfect excuse. But moving on to the second "yea but" and changing the direction of my thoughts, I stuck to my plans and discovered something enjoyable. I still had b-r-e-a-d but now I had veggies too and loved every bite.

A "yea but" can keep you stuck, frustrated, and unsatisfied or it can catapult you into something new. It all depends on how you end the sentence.

I ended mine with green peppers and a delicious new food combination that also represented an accomplishment rather than a regret.

A great way to start any day.

CHECK IN WITH YOUR INNER CHATTER

1. What is a daily habit you want to change? How can you benefit from simple strategies to help with follow-through?

2. What simple steps can you take for sticking to your new plans?

3. Would you benefit from some new thoughts to support your intentions?

IT'S YOUR STOP SIGN

"There are two primary choices in life; to
accept conditions as they exist or accept the
responsibility for changing them."
~ Denis Waitley

In a Lunch & Learn series I was leading, the participants and I were discussing the difference between thoughts and feelings. As we shared a variety of stories around personal experiences, we talked about what we think and feel and how we react when we're sitting at a red light or stop sign and someone impatiently honks their horn, sending a message of "Why didn't you go? What are you waiting for?"

Most of the group admitted to being bothered when this happens. I was one of them.

But then Jay chimed in.

Jay admitted he disliked it too but shared a new perspective he had developed for himself. He said that when this happens, he thinks to himself, "This is my stop sign." In other words, "I'm next; I'm the one pulling into traffic; it's mine to navigate."

"What a wonderful phrase and shift in thinking" I offered. "This is my stop sign."

This idea relates to almost every area of life. Change the wording to "This is my space; this is my situation; and I get to handle it the best way I see fit."

It is possible for any of us to own our space. It is also possible for us to let others own or control it.

Which one are you doing?

If you notice yourself frequently saying, "There's nothing I can do about it," then you may benefit from asking yourself this question: "Is this true or am I letting someone or something else own my space?"

Sometimes it's true that there is nothing you can do. If that's the case, it's best for you to choose strategies to help you adapt and navigate the situation.

But more often than not, saying "there's nothing I can do" is an excuse to avoid taking control of your space. When you do this, you surrender your thoughts and emotions, and therefore your actions and life's results, to someone else.

It's your space. You can own it, or you can give it away.

If you choose to own it, remind yourself that "this is my stop sign."

Now, what will you do with it?

CHECK IN WITH YOUR INNER CHATTER

1. In what ways are you letting someone else own your space by allowing them to influence your thoughts, feelings, or life results and decisions?

2. What would you need to change in order to create a sense of being in control of the choices you make?

3. What conversations would need to happen in order to make these changes?

TAKE THE FIRST STEP

"Take the first step in faith. You don't have to
see the whole staircase, just take the first step."
~ Dr. Martin Luther King Jr.

Shrimp boil.

A few years ago, my husband started to talk about how much fun it would be to make our own shrimp boil.

"Uh huh" spoken with a less than half-listening ear was my usual response. Undeterred, he mentioned it frequently. My response didn't change.

This isn't because my husband or his ideas don't matter to me. But rather, lurking beneath the surface was fear.

"Of making a shrimp boil?" you might ask. Yes.

First of all, I didn't even know what a shrimp boil was. Even after he explained, I was still uncertain (probably because of my less than half-listening ear, but we'll move on).

I didn't know what it was. And not knowing, I certainly didn't know how to make one.

It sounded difficult. And time consuming. And something we wouldn't be able to do. And where do we even start? Those were all thoughts that closed my mind to even entertaining the idea.

But here's the thing.

I didn't know anything about making a shrimp boil, so how did I know it was difficult or time consuming or that we wouldn't be able to do it?

He mentioned it again. But this time, his persistence paid off and I asked, "Can you find me a recipe?" (something he is actually quite good at doing). He agreed to do so, and I agreed to take a look.

I read through the two options he found for us and said, "This doesn't look that hard; we can definitely do this. It sounds fun."

If you find yourself avoiding something, take a moment and ask yourself, "What am I afraid of?" Then ask yourself, "If I were to do this thing, what would my first step be?" Take that first step without any promises of taking the second. That will help calm your fear and it will be easier to follow through. Then, if you choose to, move on to step two.

We made shrimp boil for the first time that year.

The next year I made it *and* shared the recipe with a friend who said, "I don't even know where to start."

"I didn't either," I said. "Try this recipe."

Shrimp boils proved to be quite easy and are now an annual tradition in our home.

All because I pushed aside my fear and took the first step.

CHECK IN WITH YOUR INNER CHATTER

1. Do you have a spouse, friend, or other important person asking you to do something, but you find yourself avoiding it? What are you afraid of? Explore your fears.

2. If you want to consider moving forward, ask yourself, "What is my first step?" Reassess your decision about whether or not to move forward *after* you take your first step.

3. Is there something you resisted doing but later discovered it was enjoyable? How can you apply this to something you currently find yourself resisting?

THE COMPARISON GAME

"The reason we struggle with insecurity is
because we compare our behind-the-scenes
with everyone else's highlight reel."
~ Steven Furtick

I was driving to a meeting and was listening to a morning show on the radio. Their topic for the day was loneliness. If you have experienced loneliness, you know the sound of its deafening silence. You know the feel of its excruciating sadness.

The show I was listening to was not a talk show. It was a show in which the host initiated a topic and listeners called in with their personal stories. One caller shared a story around navigating her pain of divorce. She offered an interesting perspective that speaks to the topic of "comparison to others." As she continued her story, she shared how she temporarily withdrew from all social media. This piqued my curiosity, and I listened closer as she described her reasoning.

At first, you might think that the access we all have to social media would be helpful. But she described how seeing other people going on vacation, enjoying dinner with friends, getting married, or sharing pictures of grandchildren was actually increasing her feelings of loneliness. In other words, being on social media made it difficult not to compare her life to the happiness she perceived in the lives of others. She found temporarily withdrawing from social media allowed her to focus on activities that helped her regain her confidence and build new friendships and relationships.

The defeat of comparing yourself to others through social media doesn't just happen around feelings of loneliness. It might be around business success, financial resources, or family circumstances, to name a few examples.

Rather than losing energy by comparing your life to someone else's, pour that energy instead into getting clarity around what you desire and focus on how to get it. Here are a few tips for moving beyond the habit of comparing yourself to others:

1. Get clear about what you want and who is helping you—and what and who are hindering you.

2. Be willing to take necessary steps even when they're difficult and uncomfortable.

3. Remember that comparison only happens in your mind, and your thoughts are one place you have complete control.

Empower your life by resisting comparison. Replace the tendency with thoughts and activities that fuel your own authenticity and uniqueness.

Focus on what brings you fulfillment.

CHECK IN WITH YOUR INNER CHATTER

1. In what area of your life do you compare yourself to someone else?

2. Is the comparison lifting you up with inspiration or dragging you down with self-chastisement?

3. What do you need to release from your life in order to stop playing the comparison game?

SEASONS OF LIFE

"What a caterpillar calls the end of the world
the master calls a butterfly." ~ Richard Bach

One day a video came up on my Facebook feed. I enjoyed watching it as it highlighted a ride named the Dragster at Cedar Point Amusement Park.

My husband and I loved going to Cedar Point when we dated in our younger years. After we reunited many years later, we were excited to return there—and we did. The Dragster was one of our many rides that day, rides that caused blood-curdling screams to pour forth from my lips. I don't think Rick screamed even once. I made up for that.

The Dragster was my hands-down favorite. After two-plus hours standing in line and alternately questioning my sanity and praying we would get enough lift on the first try not to roll backwards down the hill (yes, sometimes that happens), it was our turn. As we walked off, I looked at Rick smiling and laughing, and said, "Now that was fun."

I stopped short of saying, "Let's do it again," proving I'm not completely insane. This is in sharp contrast to the other rides of the day that elicited more of a "I can't believe I just did that" kind of reaction after exiting high and fast roller coasters the likes of which I had never experienced. Did I mention they were high—and fast?

So, remembering that day, it was fun to watch the video clip. It was even more fun to "share" it with the words "Yes, I did."

All of which brings me to my point.

Watching the video reminded me of some adventurous experiences I've had in my life, including skydiving, white water rafting, ziplining, and caving. I've also clocked quite a few miles on roller blades, and skiing was a favorite winter pastime for many years. And yes, I did ride those oh-so-high-and-fast roller coasters, even if it was only once. *Only once*, but I did ride them, and I enjoyed the experiences.

Watching the video also reminded me that for various reasons, I've elected to leave some of the adventures in my past, realizing they were for a different season of my life. And this leaves me with a choice.

I can be sad and disappointed that these are no longer a part of my life, or I can embrace the memory and be glad I got to experience them.

As we grow older, there are things we used to do but don't any longer. If we choose to be sad and depressed, that's where we'll stay—sad and depressed.

But if we remember them with joy and gratitude that they happened, we have a foundation for moving forward to the adventures still waiting for us.

Riding the Dragster might be behind me but biking and hiking still exist for me. And maybe, just maybe, that ballroom dancing will still happen. And golf lessons. And . . . well, who knows?

One thing is for certain: Plenty of fun still remains to be experienced.

CHECK IN WITH YOUR INNER CHATTER

1. What is something you experienced in your younger years but no longer do?

2. Do you embrace with gratitude that it happened or lament it's part of your past?

3. What can you focus on in your present life, so you can experience joy in the present moment?

FRONT PORCH TIME

"Life is either a daring adventure or
nothing at all." ~ Helen Keller

Our front porch.

For the first few years we lived in our home, I thought the back patio was the height of awesomeness for being outside whether relaxing or working. I never thought much about the front porch. I had a few friends comment on how relaxing and peaceful it was to which I would respond, "Uh huh, it's nice, but oh, the back patio."

I don't know when I transitioned. Maybe it was when Mom's table became our table and then became our seasonal front porch table. When it rained or was wet with dew in the morning, there was the covered front porch table. I began to venture there if for no other reason than it offered dry space on damp mornings.

For two summers now, I've spent my early morning time sitting on the front porch. I have had more moments of peace, revelation, and pure joy than I can begin to count while writing, reading, praying, or just simply sitting quietly with coffee mug in hand.

There's only one problem with the front porch: I want to stay. It is incredibly difficult to stand up and move on with my day. I resist leaving the pureness of what this time and place offers.

One day, as I was wrapping up that morning's journal writing, I wrote, "I wish I could stay on the porch." As I did, I watched an elderly neighbor walk to put some letters in her mailbox. It reminded me of an old Dan Fogelberg song titled, *Windows and Walls*, which has haunted me since the first time I heard it; the song can still bring me to tears. And I wrote, "Probably when I'm old and can stay on the porch, I'll wish I had something to do."

And with that thought, I gratefully wrote, "So today, I will joyfully get ready for work. Because today is today. Tomorrow is tomorrow. I will find joy in this day even if it means I must leave the porch waiting for me."

"But I'll be back tomorrow," I promised as I headed off to shower.

I'll be back tomorrow.

CHECK IN WITH YOUR INNER CHATTER

1. Do you lament everyday realities like, "I have to go to work" or "Oh, wow, it's Monday again"?

2. Each time you notice a negative perspective around an everyday reality, chose to shift to gratitude. What are you thankful for in that scenario?

3. What can you do to establish a habit of being in gratitude throughout your day?

PARASAILING . . . FINALLY

"Twenty years from now you will be more
disappointed by the things that you didn't do
then by the ones you did do. So throw off the
bowlines. Sail away from the safe harbor. Catch
the trade winds in your sails. Explore. Dream.
Discover." ~ Mark Twain

I had long wanted to go parasailing.

I had jumped out of an airplane. Incredibly scary.
And, although hard to believe, it was also anti-climactic.

I've also been skiing which I loved; roller blading
which was my constant through one incredibly difficult
summer; and caving, which I'm glad I experienced when I
was much younger and, to be honest, thinner.

I've gone ziplining which was way scarier for others
than it was for me. I thoroughly enjoyed floating from tree
stand to tree stand.

So why not parasailing?

Each time I traveled for a beach vacation, I said I
would. However, each time I came home, I hadn't.

Then my husband and I started to do the same thing.
"This year let's go parasailing" we would say. And each time
we would come home saying, "Why didn't we?"

Until one year when we did indeed choose, and very
much enjoyed, the adventure.

So, why was that year different?

We set an intention. Before leaving for vacation, we
committed that parasailing would be our "try something
new" activity for that year's trip. And, as soon as we arrived,

we decided on which company we would use, what day and time we wanted to go, and called to reserve our spot.

In other words, we set an intention *including an action plan.*

Sometimes the difference between doing something and not doing it has nothing to do with money, time, or energy. It doesn't reflect whether or not there was available opportunity. When we are honest with ourselves, most times it simply has to do with making a choice.

That year, rather than coming home asking, "Why didn't we?", we came home talking about how much fun we had. We traded comments about our favorite part of the ride (mine was the take-off from the boat) and how close we got to the dolphins. We swear they were performing just for us.

We came home with a memory rather than a regret.

A memory that started by setting our intention.

CHECK IN WITH YOUR INNER CHATTER

1. What is something you've long said you want to do but have never done?

2. When is the next time that activity will be a possibility?

3. What steps can you take to ensure it becomes a reality rather than a regret?

REACTING VS. RESPONDING

"I alone cannot change the world, but I can cast a stone across the waters to create many ripples." ~ Mother Teresa

There are some things that frustrate me in daily life. My phone is one of them.

Being a small computer that I think knows more about my life than I do, it frequently prompts me to turn on my location. Some of these prompts I understand, like when I want to use it as my GPS. My phone needs to know where I am to guide me in getting where I want to go. Simple enough.

Other times, it just isn't necessary. For me at least.

Like the time I was checking weather and was prompted to turn on cookies in my browser so "it" could know my location. "Right there," I said. "Beaver Falls; if I want a different city, I'll be sure to put in a new one; when I'm interested in changing it, I'll be sure to let you know" I continued telling (yelling at?) my phone.

I waited for my husband to contribute to this tongue lashing, but he didn't. In his silent response, I was convicted. He didn't tell me I was wrong; he didn't criticize me. He just simply and quietly didn't engage. That was a good thing. It caused me to think about my words and, more importantly, my tone.

I didn't like what I heard coming out of my mouth. Frustration. Complaining. Bitter tone. I didn't like hearing myself and figured it hadn't sounded pleasant to my husband either. I was thankful he quietly continued what he was doing.

"I'm sorry" I said. "I know that sounded crabby and

not much fun to be around."

He stayed quiet for another moment, and then he said, "Those things bother me too; I just focus on not letting them get to me."

I was reminded of something I read not long ago that stated, "You don't have to react to everything that bothers you. You get to choose."

I. Get. To. Choose.

My first choice is in using a smart phone. It would be difficult to navigate our current world without one, but it is still my decision.

My second choice is in leaving my location off which causes my phone to prompt me in the first place.

And third, and maybe the most important one for me, is I get to choose my reaction. This is the one that directs the energy I surround myself with; it creates what I contribute to my environment.

Yes, our phones want to know our location. But only I, and you, have the choice as to what energy we pour into that location.

If I want to be in places that are loving, peaceful, and renewing, then I must contribute that energy. It starts with me.

And the reaction I choose.

CHECK IN WITH YOUR INNER CHATTER

1. Do you notice yourself being snippy with inanimate objects? How does it make you feel?

2. Take a moment to ask yourself, "Is there something deeper that is the real cause of my frustration?"

3. What is needed to process and manage the deeper cause of your frustration? Only when you manage the deeper issue will you truly be able to let go of stress and contribute positive energy to your environment.

SEEKING HARMONY

"But what is happiness except the simple
harmony between a man and the life he leads?"
~ Albert Camus

I love my quiet time, my alone time, my me-time spent completely by myself when I get to relax, regroup, and rejuvenate. My husband is not so much that way. He doesn't value alone and quiet time the way I do.

I could think "There's something wrong with me that I need that when he doesn't" but I don't. He could think "She doesn't want to spend time with me" but he doesn't. We each have different things that we value, and we accept and respect that in each other.

In life, there are a variety of relationships that make up your personal world. There are spouses and other intimate partners; there are family and friends, co-workers, and people in your social and community networks. There are business relationships with people you serve and those who serve you. Certainly, in all of these, there are similarities. Without a doubt, there are also differences.

In order to create a calm and harmonious lifestyle, it's important to recognize and respect what's important to you. It is also important to cultivate a willingness to accept and respect what is important to others.

Rather than letting your differences become a source of stress or worry for you, seek to discover a way to honor both what you value—and what they value. It's not a question of a "right" way or a "wrong" way. It's a matter of what works best for each of you and how those flow together in harmony.

If my husband and I didn't choose to respect and

honor our differences around quiet time, it would cause disagreements and unnecessary misunderstandings in our relationship. But we like peace in our lives and so we choose to make peace happen for us.

There is nothing I love more than spending time with my husband—except when what I want most is to be alone. Then I'm glad he has golf. And I have my book.

Harmony.

CHECK IN WITH YOUR INNER CHATTER

1. Do you prefer to rest, rejuvenate, and re-energize alone or in the company of others?

2. What are your favorite activities that allow your mind to rest?

3. Do you allow yourself these opportunities? Why or why not?

MOM–ISMS

"It doesn't matter which side of the fence you get off on sometimes. What matters most is getting off. You cannot make progress without making a decision. ~ Jim Rohn

Mom wisdom—wise pieces of advice shared by moms everywhere. We, of course, don't understand or like these when we're young. It's only as we mature that we realize the wisdom in their words. I remember many from my mom.

Probably because of my dislike for making decisions, I heard this one quite often: "You make the best decision you can at the time you're making it; and then, you don't look back."

I remembered these words recently when I realized that I, a friend, a family member, and a client were all making important decisions.

Mom's advice was wise. But what else can you do to support your decision process? Here are three I have found valuable:

1. Clarity: To make the best decision possible, start by getting clarity around what you want. Consider what you want for yourself and for important others.

2. Trust in God and self: Even when you value placing your trust in God, your confidence in moving forward comes with trusting yourself to follow where He leads. And it's critical that you believe in yourself to make wise, well-thought-out decisions. Also know that

if things don't turn out as planned, you have the intelligence and skills to shift as needed.

3. Communication: There will be people you must talk to about your decision. They may—or may not—react well. Remind yourself this doesn't dictate whether or not your decision is a good one.

When you have a decision to make, the worst thing you can do is stand still. This will leave you stressed, frustrated, and stuck. Your time and energy will be spent on analyzing rather than doing.

Support your decision-making process by focusing on clarity, trust, and communication.

Then, make the best decision you can at the time you're making it.

And look forward.

Thanks, Mom.

CHECK IN WITH YOUR INNER CHATTER

1. What is your decision-making style? Do you make quick decisions, forging ahead toward results? Or are you more analytical, thinking through all possibilities before making a decision?

2. Do you trust yourself when making a decision? Why or why not?

3. How do you make God a part of your decision-making process?

BEYOND A PLUMBING PROBLEM

"We must stop regarding unpleasant or
unexpected things as interruptions of real life.
The truth is that interruptions are real life."
~ C.S. Lewis

For a short time, we were using our downstairs bathroom because the tile in our primary shower was being replaced. One morning, as I walked out of the room after my shower, I discovered water had backed up into the laundry room.

"Hmm", I said to no one but the empty room, "I wonder what that is?"

When my husband woke up, I told him, "We have a problem." Because, you know, everyone loves to wake up to the words, "We have a problem."

"What's up" he calmly asked. Yes, he was calm—not a surprise. And so was I.

I went on to explain about the water back-up in the laundry room. We then methodically discussed our options, soon realizing the solution was beyond our skill level for plumbing. First, I would call the home warranty company and request an appointment for a plumber. Then we went on to plan our day in a way that I wouldn't miss any clients. And, if needed, he would work from home.

By the time later in the day when our plumbing was fixed, I hadn't missed any clients and he had worked a couple of hours from home. We experienced a smooth transition from problem to implemented solutions with barely a blip on the radar of our daily life.

All that led me to ask the questions, "Why not this same level of peace and calm with day in, day out issues?" and "Why do I let myself get more overwhelmed with simple everyday decisions?"

Taking the time to sit and plan was the clear answer to both questions.

On the days that I make a concrete plan, I accomplish more, and I keep up with the most important tasks. At the end of the day, I might be tired, but I'm satisfied with my day and I'm ready for the next one.

But on the days that I don't make a specific plan, I flounder. I figure out what fire to put out next and then move on to the next one. At the end of those days, I'm exhausted, stressed, and even anxious. I struggle to re-fuel even after a night's sleep. I wake up the next day with my mind spinning like an amusement park ride.

The trick I've learned to implement is to take ten minutes each morning to plan the rest of my day—to identify my intentions for the specific things I want to accomplish.

A few minutes of planning can positively impact the course of any day.

Even if there's dirty water backing up in the basement.

CHECK IN WITH YOUR INNER CHATTER

1. What are three ways that setting a daily and weekly plan provides value?

2. Are you a morning person or more of a night owl? Utilize this awareness to establish a habit of setting aside ten minutes of planning time each day.

3. What is something you can do to stay calm and focused when unexpected events happen that interrupt your plan?

FEAR: FALSE EVIDENCE OR REAL DANGER?

"He has not learned the lesson of life who does
not every day surmount a fear."
~ Ralph Waldo Emerson

I have attended churches over the years where I became fond of the pastor's sermon style. The ones I always liked the most opened their message with a story. As people, we relate to stories, and they help us process life—both the good and the difficult.

On one memorable occasion, the pastor presented a sermon on fear that started with a wonderfully humorous story about discovering a snake in his basement. I don't think he found it humorous in the moment he found that slithering, slimy, creepy reptile (Can you guess how I feel about snakes?). But this man knew how to tell an engaging story. I think I cried tears of laughter that day.

He went on to say that fear exists in our lives as a warning that "there is danger there." (Have you noticed how fear and snake stories just seem to go hand in hand?)

In contrast, I have also often heard that FEAR is an acronym for False Evidence Appearing Real. There are times that we experience feelings of fear when nothing dangerous or potentially harmful exists in that moment. This type of fear holds us back from action that we want or need to take. It can stop us in our tracks just like seeing a snake on our path—even though stopping is not necessary or even the most beneficial thing to do.

Sometimes the challenge is knowing which of these messages is truth. Is there danger? Or is it false evidence appearing real?

Or is there a different message altogether?

Without a doubt, fear can be a gift. It is something to be acknowledged and something for which we can be thankful because it exists to teach us a lesson. Fear is there to send us a message. When we cultivate a habit of acknowledging our fears with, "Thank you for the message you bring" and "What are showing me?", then fear indeed becomes a great gift.

How can you utilize this gift in your life?

One significant way fear is a gift is when it signals to you, "There is knowledge, skill, or education that will be of benefit to you to help you move forward."

Sometimes fear is not there to say, "Don't do that." Sometimes fear is simply there to say, "Wait, there's something else for you to learn before you do that" or "There is something for you to do differently. Think about it before you move forward."

Cultivate the habit of acknowledging your fear, being thankful for it, and then asking "What are you here to teach me?"

I think I will always be afraid of snakes. I suspect the pastor will be as well. The thing I'm not afraid of is learning something new.

But I only know it's needed when I pause and ask, "What are you here to teach me?"

CHECK IN WITH YOUR INNER CHATTER

1. What is something you want to do but fear is holding you back?

2. Take time to journal about what you want and what your fear is. As you do, notice if there is a valid reason for your fear or if its false evidence appearing real.

3. During your time of journaling, notice also if new, creative action steps are coming to mind. Are you experiencing a nudge that says, "Try this"? The best way beyond your fear is through it. Those steps coming to mind just might be your steps through to the other side.

THE ATTENTION WE PAY TO FEAR

"Courage is not about being fearless – it's about owning your fear and using it to move you forward, to give you strength." ~ Michael Port

As I stated in a previous story, I don't like snakes. Hate is probably a more accurate word.

Wait, let me start over.

I say I hate snakes when what I really mean is that I'm afraid of them. I think being afraid of snakes is a healthy fear and I'm good with it. I have no desire to learn about them or otherwise find a way not to be afraid of them.

Or do I?

If by afraid I mean I won't touch one, won't be assertive around one, and will always make a wide path steering clear (very, very clear) of one, then yes, I'm good with that.

But what if my fear prevents me from doing things I enjoy because I'm afraid I "might" see one? What if my fear

- prevents me from tending to our garden because one could be hiding in the ground cover?
- makes me hesitant to hike in the woods because I might come across one?
- interferes with my joy while bike riding because I'm anxiously on the lookout for one?

These things are real struggles for me. This means I'm letting my fear that I might, maybe, could possibly see one interfere with things I want to be doing. Did you notice the words: *might, maybe, could possibly*?

Here's the thing. I just celebrated my sixtieth

birthday. And, outside of the zoo or in pictures, I've seen two snakes in my lifetime. Two. And neither of them paid one iota of attention to me.

All of which makes me think about fear and how it stops us from doing the very things we most want to be doing.

Is there something you want to do in your life or business, but fear inhibits you? What difference would it make in your life if you acted despite your fear?

It is certainly a possibility that I will see a snake again someday. It is also likely that this one will pay no more attention to me than the first two did. So, what is stopping me—or you—from doing the things we want to do?

Nothing but a thought, a thought of what might, maybe, could possibly happen. We each also have the power to think, "It might not." And "it might not" will totally change the actions we're willing to take.

It is likely I will always be afraid of snakes. But I can choose how I let that fear interfere with my life.

The bike path, the hike, and the garden call my name every spring.

I look forward to saying, "Yes, as a matter of fact, I will."

CHECK IN WITH YOUR INNER CHATTER

1. What do you want to do in your life but fear stops you?

2. What actions would you take if you changed your thoughts to, "What if that doesn't happen; what would I do?"

3. Commit to taking one action step today toward fulfilling your dream. When you discover the "snake didn't bite you," you'll cultivate more courage to take the next step.

FLIP THE SWITCH

"Don't just pray for God to open doors, pray for
God to close doors in your life that need to be
closed." ~ Joyce Meyer

We have an exhaust fan in our bathroom that annoys me. I can't exactly tell you why because I don't actually know. The former speech pathologist in me says the pitch of the sound is offensive to my sensory system. The rest of me says, "It really doesn't matter; that sound is just so unnerving."

Every morning, I turn it on and at first, I don't pay it much mind. I'm okay while I'm in the shower. The sound of the water must either muffle the sound or it calms me.

But then I turn the water off and I can feel my tension rising as I go through the rest of my routine. I've just had a hot, soothing, and mind-clearing shower and it's about to be undone by *that sound*. I could easily morph into the Grinch with my mind screaming, "All the noise, all the noise, noise, noise, *noise!*"

When this first happened, I tried to ignore it. Then I attempted to logically manage it by saying, "Come on, Lisa, it's just an exhaust fan; it's not a big deal." When that didn't work, I tried a few mindfulness techniques like deep breaths and calm thoughts.

Now you might already be thinking, "Why didn't you just turn it off?"

In truth, I didn't even consider turning it off. My routine was having it on, and I didn't think to consider any other option. When I did give it a moment's thought, I would reason to myself, "The mirror will fog."

And then one day—one oh so fine day— I thought,

"Why don't you just wipe the mirror with a towel?" I asked myself, "Seriously, Lisa, does it really matter all that much if you learn to 'mindfully manage' this sound? Why not just eliminate it by turning off the fan when you step out of the shower?"

As a coach and in my own personal philosophy, I'm all about managing life stress in ways that empower us rather than defeat us. And oftentimes, eliminating the cause of stress isn't an option. And so, other options must be discovered.

But there are also times that eliminating the source of stress is the best option.

"But I can't because . . ." you might say; or "Well, that's a simple story about an exhaust fan but my situation is . . ." And you may be right.

On the other hand, you may be holding on to something that you can let go of. It may have become a part of your routine and you hold on to it because you just haven't considered letting it go.

I challenge you today to look at what is causing stress in your life. Are you tolerating something stressful when you could eliminate it instead?

You can keep tolerating it. Or, like our exhaust fan, you can shut it off instead.

Flip the switch. The relief is real.

CHECK IN WITH YOUR INNER CHATTER

1. What are the stressors in your life?

2. Are you tolerating a stressor when instead you could eliminate it?

3. Identify action steps you can take to remedy rather than tolerate the stressor.

THE CLOCK ON
THE WALL

"Habit is habit, and not to be flung out of the window by any man but coaxed downstairs a step at a time." ~ Mark Twain

From January through August, we have a large clock that hangs on the wall in our family room. But in the fall, a large wreath hangs in its place. Then comes December and, well, you would just have to see the winter wonderland my husband creates for the holidays. It's a beautiful, wintery scene with trees, carolers, and a holiday glow. But there's no clock on the wall. He's the decorator in our family and he's good at it. I don't question—or mind—the absence of the clock.

But when it's hanging, that clock is in an optimally functional location. Whether I'm in the kitchen, watching TV, reading in the family room, or simply going up and down our stairs, I can always count on seeing what time it is. I can count on it . . . until September that is.

By early September, our home is decorated with the nurturing and comforting feel of the autumn season and from that time through early January, we are without the clock on the wall. For about three weeks, I continue to look at that wall to see what time it is. It takes me three weeks before I even begin to remember the clock is not there. By week four, I begin to remember but still only as my head is turning and gets halfway there. It takes several weeks until I am consistently remembering to look elsewhere for the time.

I've heard it said that it takes 21 to 30 days to change

a habit. Experience tells me it takes even longer. It took me a full month to remember that a clock was no longer hanging on our wall. It has taken longer than that to change more serious, long-standing habits (food and sleep patterns to mention just two of them).

Have you ever tried to change a habit and found yourself quickly lamenting, "Well, this plan isn't working"? Consider this idea that it takes 21 to 30-plus days to change a habit and ask yourself, "Have I given my plan sufficient time to become a new habit?"

I know you have had experiences similar to my clock story. We've all laughed as we shared the stories with others. You accept them as being a part of life—the way things are and the way your mind works. You never question that it takes time to adapt to these new scenarios.

We can all laugh when it's the clock on the wall, but as you move forward in life, embrace the time needed to adapt to new and more meaningful life-changing habits.

Today is day one.

CHECK IN WITH YOUR INNER CHATTER

1. What is a habit you have long stated you want to change?

2. What are three small but measurable action steps you can implement to shift your habit?

3. Identify triggers that will remind you to use your new behavior. For example, would an alarm or a visual cue be helpful?

HELP WANTED

"Ask for help. Not because you are weak but
because you want to remain strong."
~ Les Brown

In my role as a life coach, I often have one-on-one meetings over coffee or lunch as part of my business networking.

On one occasion, I was meeting with a young woman who is a licensed counselor and owns her own private practice. We met a few years earlier and occasionally bumped into each other at other networking events. We enjoyed each other's company and found it mutually beneficial to learn about the similarities and differences between counseling and coaching with a goal of making referrals to each other. But on this day, we transitioned into sharing with each other around personal challenges we were each facing.

As a licensed counselor and a life coach, we spend our days helping others through life's challenges. And yet, we find when it comes to ourselves, we also benefit from seeking the counsel of another professional. We seek the guidance of someone else even when our own circumstances are like the ones experienced by our clients.

It doesn't take being a coach or a counselor to grasp this feeling or experience. Think about a time you helped a friend or family member and shared wise words and suggestions that benefited them greatly. But you couldn't apply the same wisdom when you were facing an equivalent trial in your own life. You may have even thought, "I helped so and so, why can't I do this for myself?"

Everyone, including me, you, and my friend

mentioned above, benefits from outside perspectives. But there's a sticking point to this. It takes being vulnerable. You must be willing to say, "I need help with this."

Experience tells me that asking for help is a sensitive subject for most people. Even the thought of it is a breeding ground for inner chatter. Consider the flurry of anxious and worry-filled thoughts you have as you consider something that touches your vulnerability nerve; thoughts like, *They'll think I'm not capable; I should be able to handle this; I'll look stupid if I ask for help.* Even more frightening are the thoughts, *They won't like me. I'll lose their friendship.*

How often would you benefit from allowing the help, guidance, or assistance of others but still you don't reach out and ask?

In order to move yourself forward in life and in whatever area you're struggling, you must be able to set aside the voice that says, "If you can't handle this, you're not good enough" and be willing to say instead, "This is difficult for me; I need help."

Your value doesn't come in being able to manage all of life on your own.

Your greatest value to you and to others will come when you're willing to say, "I need help with this."

CHECK IN WITH YOUR INNER CHATTER

1. Is there something in your life causing stress, frustration, sadness, or other difficult emotions?

2. Who can you talk with about this situation? Consider both professional and non-professional options.

3. Make the call today to schedule an appointment to chat.

INTUITION WORKS— UNTIL IT DOESN'T

"Only in the darkness can you see the stars."
~ Dr. Martin Luther King Jr.

When I was in my teens, I recognized that I had strong intuition. It would seem like I knew things before they happened. I'm not talking big things like world-changing events; and fortunately, I'm also not talking about seeing my future career as a psychic.

I am talking about things in my own life such as looking forward to something that was planned and yet "knowing" it wasn't going to happen—and it wouldn't; or hoping for something specific to happen and yet knowing it wasn't going to—and again, it wouldn't.

At the time, I didn't call it intuition. In fact, I didn't know what to call it. Many people told me it was "just coincidence." I knew it wasn't— this was different. I stopped telling people. I also harbored a quiet anxiety that I was somehow weird and quite possibly just a little crazy. I literally prayed to lose this thing I didn't understand.

I still have a strong intuitive awareness in my life. Over the years, I've come to believe that intuition is a way that God communicates with us. We see, hear, or think something and we just simply "know." It's like a whisper in our heart. These are the times God has decided to let me have a sneak peek at a coming event; or it's a time that He needs me to know, "Go in this direction."

But God, being God, doesn't *always* do this. Sometimes He just leaves me out there hanging. Words like trust, belief, and faith come to mind right now. Sometimes

I don't have any knowing whatsoever. That's right: none, zilch, zip. It's not that I don't want it, mind you; I just simply don't have it.

What happens to us when there's the future looming ahead and we don't know what it's going to bring; when we don't have an answer we desire; when we don't know what an outcome is going to be? Without a doubt, we are primed for worry.

We worry because we want to predict, determine, or know what the future will bring. We want to know what decision to make a day, a week, or a month from now; we want to know what to do in response to any and all possible future scenarios. We want answers to all of our what-ifs and worry is one way we try to get them.

Worry responses are activated when our intuition tells us something isn't going to be the way we want it to be and so, we want to change it. We worry when we don't have any intuitive awareness and we want to predict the future; and we want to predict it *with accuracy*.

In either case, worry doesn't work. Worry, no matter how much of it we do, will never change anything, or show us something it's not yet time for us to know. To live a life of peace and balance, this is a fact we must accept.

I now welcome my intuition knowing it is a gift; it has a purpose. The times my intuitive awareness is absent are also a gift; this also has a purpose. It's the same for you.

Sometimes we have intuitive awareness; sometimes we don't. That's why we're also given the ability to trust, believe, and have faith. With these gifts, we can have confidence that we will handle the future, both the good and the bad of it, one day and one step at a time.

You can worry. Or you have faith and trust in a powerful God who has promised to ride through that journey with you.

Choose the one that brings peace.

CHECK IN WITH YOUR INNER CHATTER

1. Do you recognize your own intuitive awareness?

2. Do you trust yourself to hear and discern when God is speaking to you? If not, what stops you?

3. What are you doing on a daily basis to cultivate your trust and faith in God?

A LESSON MORE IMPORTANT THAN THE RESULT

"A man cannot be comfortable without his
own approval." ~ Mark Twain

When I was settling Mom's estate, we ran into an issue with her auto lease. But let me start the story a year before she died.

Mom had found a car she liked and wanted to lease. Among the conservative silver and blue choices, she pointed to a red one and said, "I want that one." All 84 years of her wanted the red one. I still smile at the memory.

My husband and I went with her to see the vehicle and finalize the paperwork. We both remember her asking one specific question.

"What if something happens to me and I die before the lease time expires?"

"Your family just needs to bring the vehicle back to the dealership," she was told.

As painful as it was to consider, I knew the possibility of her passing before the lease expired was real. I listened more intently than I may have had this ever-present possibility not existed.

She furthered questioned the remaining payments and was told, "They just need to bring the vehicle back and that will be the end of it." She asked multiple times. The salesman answered the same multiple times. I reiterated the question and answer as confirmation. There was no change.

Mom did die before the lease expired. We were

diligent in returning the vehicle quickly. The salesman was there and verbally confirmed we had done what was needed. He initialed a paper indicating the vehicle had been returned to them.

"Yes, that's all you need to do," he confirmed.

And so, it was complete. We thought.

But then we received multiple letters and phone calls from the company's collections department. Each time I talked with them I was told the same thing: We had done what was needed and to ignore the letters.

Until it was no longer in the hands of the vehicle company but had been turned over to a collection agency. And the attorney settling Mom's estate said they were a legitimate collection agency and yes, we did indeed need to pay off the amount owed on the lease that now included some hefty fees and penalties.

I called the car company and vehemently argued with them. I called the dealership. I called a second attorney. In the end, I wrote a check out of the estate account and paid the balance owed. I did so begrudgingly and with much anger, but I paid it.

Did I win? No. And yes.

I didn't win the argument and to this day I believe I was right. But yes, I also did because I fought the case. I spoke up and argued for what I believed was right. I made my opinion known. Most importantly, I fought for Mom who was misled by the salesman and who could no longer fight for herself.

And, if I hadn't fought, I would have walked away forever mad at myself for not speaking up. I would have regretted not being bolder for what I believed. I would have always questioned my decision to stay quiet. So, no I didn't win the argument. But what I did win was more important.

I won the courage to speak.

I like to think Mom was rooting for me.

She always did.

CHECK IN WITH YOUR INNER CHATTER

1. When faced with an intimidating situation, do you speak up or bury your thoughts and feelings?

2. What fears do you hold when you consider being bold sharing your thoughts, opinions, or wants/needs?

3. What new thought can you focus on to replace your self-sabotaging inner chatter?

NO LOOKING BACK

"Glory days happen to the degree we
trust God." ~ Max Lucado

I once listened to a sermon that began with a snippet
from Bruce Springsteen's video of *Glory Days*. Yes, it happened in church.

I don't have glory days. In fact, I have lived pretty
much the opposite. I regret many of the choices I made in my
early teenage years, high school, and college. In full disclosure, I have significant regrets around decisions I made well
into my adult years when one would believe I "should have
known better." These choices haunted me for years and I must
remain cautious that I don't allow them to continue to do so.

My turn-around point came when I cultivated a new
perspective which happened in my 58th year.

Until I was in my late (very late) forties, I struggled to
figure out exactly what would bring the satisfaction and fulfillment I was seeking. The longer I lived without it, the more I
was haunted by what I thought of as "all of my past mistakes."
I could start many conversations with the words, "If only I
had (or hadn't)." This was usually followed by something like,
"Why was I so stupid" or "I should have known better."

I know people who went to college to study for what
would become their lifelong career. They got married; they
had families. For all these years it would seem they "had it
all together." I've admired them through the years and in
many ways, I still do. But the more I compared myself to
them, the worse I felt about my own choices.

Then my new perspective arrived.

Yes, I may have stumbled. I even completely fell
sometimes—really hard painful falls. Many of these falls

came in the wake of my saying, "I knew I shouldn't have" or "Something inside me knew not to do that."

But, as a good friend reminded me, they were all a part of my journey. And, every time I fell, I got up and tried again. Through it all, I refused to give up. I knew that what I was looking for was available to me and I kept searching.

And now I'm looking forward to the best years of my life. I'm excited about what is before me. I'm in no hurry to reach retirement. I'm not wondering, "What will I do with myself now that I'm retired?" I'm fully embracing my future and that excites me.

I love being a life coach and by this, I mean I fully and completely love what I do; it fills my heart and fuels my days. I love sharing new perspectives with others through my writings. I get an adrenaline rush when I speak in front of an audience and feedback tells me I've reached someone—or many someones.

There are many people who regret the past as I did. If you're one of them, choose to shift your perspective. See your past as part of your journey; view each choice as a lesson you needed to learn. Let go of your guilt and shame.

Now instead of bemoaning and regretting my past and feeling the need to justify and explain my choices, I look at my present and my future.

I tell people about those instead.

My glory days yet to come.

CHECK IN WITH YOUR INNER CHATTER

1. Do you have regrets from your past that you're still holding on to?

2. How can you reframe that experience into a lesson learned?

3. What new adventures and experiences do you want to create for your future? What steps can be taken today to help you pursue that dream?

LET'S JUST SLEEP IN

"Each day the Lord pours His unfailing love
upon me." ~ Psalm 42:8

After Mom died, I got into the habit most mornings of over-sleeping. It wasn't a huge problem, but it happened often enough that I was aware of it. I'm okay with that because it was just what I needed.

But after some time had passed, I said quietly to myself one night, "Tomorrow morning I will get up when I wake up" (rather than roll over and go back to sleep); and I did.

I didn't do this because I thought I "should" or "had to." There was no pressure from anyone, including myself, to do so. I simply wanted to do it.

I wanted to because moving on with my life is what Mom would want me to do. Soon after she passed, she let me know that she was in a good place now. In fact, her clear message to me was, "I'm where I need to be now." And as much as I long for her place to be here with me, I don't get that choice.

And so, amidst the sadness of missing her, I decided that I would start by getting up early because that is what I do.

The first (well, almost first) thing I did that day was make my morning cup of coffee and head to my quiet place for reading a daily meditation and journaling. I usually read first but that day I chose to write first and in doing so, I wrote that I wanted to make it a good day.

And then I read my daily meditation and was reminded that I am not alone in this journey. I realized that when I wrote that I wanted to make it a better day, I did so with self will and determination. And then I read and was reminded, "You are not alone; I am God, and I am with you always."

And I remembered. My shoulders relaxed. I took a calmer and deeper breath. And I moved on with my day.

Everyone needs a foundation on which to live. My foundation is my faith and trust in God.

Slowly but quite certainly, I transitioned back to choosing to set my alarm and get up at my intended time. I re-arranged how I managed each morning. But whether it's a "get ready and head out the door" type of morning or one that I am able to extend my morning habits a little longer, I always start with one thing. I reaffirm my trust and faith in God.

Not because God needs it.

Because I do.

CHECK IN WITH YOUR INNER CHATTER

1. Do you have a regular morning routine that helps you ground your day from the start, so you are focused and armed with a positive perspective?

2. What do you do when affirming your trust and faith in God is needed?

3. What other routines help you stay grounded when life is messy, uncertain, and sad?

CHOOSING A NEW PATH

"Do not go where the path may lead, go instead
where there is no path and leave a trail."
~ Ralph Waldo Emerson

It was a holiday weekend and my husband and I had decided to go biking. Since it is one of our favorite ways to spend a day, this is a common choice for us. The thing that is not so common is for us to pick a trail we have not been on previously.

It's easy to stay with trails that are familiar to us. We know where we'll park, and we know what to expect in terms of intensity. We know what the terrain will be like and whether there are any sections where we'll need to bike on the road. We have enough information to plan our mileage and how much time we need. And we know important things like how far to the next "Porta-John." Okay, that one's for me.

The point is that it's easy to stay with what we know, with what is familiar to us. But on this particular weekend, we ventured to a new trail. In going beyond the familiar, we discovered an incredibly fun and renewing experience.

We biked through beautiful woods and a quaint little town. We discovered an antique shop and several farm markets. We loved the ride and quickly made plans to go back to this path again.

As we rode that day, I thought about how often we function much the same in life, staying with what's familiar, known, and safe.

How often do you do what is familiar and safe? How

often do you keep doing the same things even when you know something new could bring more satisfying results?

When you are willing to venture out and try something new, you often discover greater satisfaction and fulfillment. You discover a life that is aligned with the authenticity of your adventurous heart. If you find yourself doing the same things again and again in some area of your life and you're frustrated by your results, maybe it's time to do something different. Maybe it's time to try a new trail.

CHECK IN WITH YOUR INNER CHATTER

1. Is repeatedly falling into the same dull routine frustrating you and leaving you disappointed and unfulfilled? In what area(s) of your life is this occurring?

2. Now that you've identified the area(s), what is something new and adventurous you'd like to try?

3. Make a commitment. Consider these factors: who will be involved? What do you want to do? When will you do it? Where will you go? Then schedule it!

SELF-SABOTAGE?

"Find out where joy resides and give it a voice
far beyond singing. For to miss the joy is to
miss all." ~ Robert Louis Stevenson

I was coming home from some meetings with clients and had two errands to do along the way, one of which was at Home Depot. As I walked toward the garden section, I was drawn to some beautiful fall mums. I'm not sure which color I loved the most, but I believe it was the yellow ones—such a beautiful bright color that gave me joy just looking at them.

I had been watching a neighbor down the road begin to add fall flowers around her home. Each time I'd see something new I would think, "Wow, I really want to put some mums around our house this year." And so, it would seem that my discovery at Home Depot was the perfect intersection between my love for fall mums and my wish to plant them—except for one thing.

Each year, I talk about how much I love these fall beauties. Every August I start saying, "I'm going to plant them 'this year.'" And every year when November rolls around, I tell myself, "Definitely next year."

As I enjoyed a few moments of roaming around all the sizes and colors, it started. "It's only August, you don't need them yet; you don't know how many you need or what sizes; what colors would look best? You better think about this first; you can come back later and get them." That was all going through my head even as I enjoyed walking around.

But then I decided to resist what was trying to take my mind captive. A few moments of choosing size and another few visualizing which colors would look best and where, and there I was, adding them to my shopping cart. Just thinking of how beautiful they would look around our landscape released in me a freedom and sense of joy.

As a woman and as a coach, I find many of us have difficulty allowing ourselves some of the simple joys of life. If we're not doing something to help someone else or we're spending money on something that cannot be defined as a "need," it is easy to procrastinate and justify why it is not important to do this or that. But in our heart we know we want to do it. In other words, we sabotage and deprive ourselves of simple pleasures.

Can you identify with this type of sabotage thinking?

For many years, I let this kind of inner chatter cheat me out of the things I most enjoy in life. Fortunately, I have learned to argue back with another voice. It's a stronger one. It affirms my value and my worth. It allows me, as I nurture and care for others, to put myself into my life equation as well.

Because I love flowers and I especially love fall mums, that year I let myself enjoy them rather than walk away with all the reasons I would do it another day. It took some concentration. I had to push aside all of the sabotage that was stomping around in my mind.

The beauty that surrounded our home as our temperatures turned cooler was worth the effort.

As was the joy I felt each time I pulled in the driveway.

CHECK IN WITH YOUR INNER CHATTER

1. What is a simple pleasure in your life you don't allow yourself to enjoy?

2. Reflect on, "What are my deep, inner thoughts that won't allow me to have that thing?"

3. In what way can you reframe your answer to #2 so you give yourself permission to enjoy simple pleasures in life?

THE PLACES
YOU FIND JOY

"We find such delight in the joy of children that
our hearts become too big for our bodies."
~ Kim Anderson

After my husband and I completed one of our biking
journeys, we went to eat brunch at a great Amish restaurant.
On our way out, I stopped to use the restroom and in there
was a young girl and her mom. I knew this not because I
could see them, but because the little girl was happily singing as she did what she came there to do.

Singing. Happily and joyfully singing. I could hear
her smile.

As the typical parental words of, "Okay, we have
to wash your hands" were uttered, the girl exclaimed with
great enthusiasm, "I'll do it" (as in, "I'll do it by myself"). It
was said with an equal amount of excitement as her singing
had been just a few moments earlier. In her voice, I could
hear her skipping to the sink.

It all made me smile and I commented to her mom
about the child's happiness and joy and how much I enjoyed
them. The little girl beamed. (Then asked her mom on the
way out, "Who was that lady?")

Children find delight in just about everything. And
when we notice, it causes us to smile. Why do we lose this
as adults? This ability to find joy in the simple things of life
that is.

I can guarantee you won't find me singing in public
restrooms and I don't get a surge of excitement just because
it's time to wash my hands. But there is so much else in a day

that opens the possibility of discovering joy when we open our eyes to it.

There's the hug of a friend or spouse; the feel of the sun or breeze on our skin; laughter; a favorite food; the first sip of morning coffee—or a small child you don't even know who sings and laughs about, well, just about anything. You just have to pause long enough to realize they're there.

When you choose, you can be as a young child and find joy in everyday life. Don't wait for the big vacation, the weekend, or a holiday. Resist thinking it will come "tomorrow" when today's painful experience has lessened its grip on your emotions. You will go a long way to reducing your feelings of stress and toward living with a greater sense of satisfaction and fulfillment when you choose to see and appreciate the wonders that show themselves in everyday life.

Where will you find joy today?

You will recognize it when your "heart becomes too big for your body."

CHECK IN WITH YOUR INNER CHATTER

1. Name ten things in everyday life that bring you a sense of joy.

2. Set specific times each day that you commit to thinking of simple joys. For example, you can do so as you drive to work, prepare for sleep, or while completing a daily task such as cleaning up the kitchen.

3. With each simple joy you discover, utter the words "thank you."

WHERE EVERYBODY KNOWS YOUR NAME

"The path to belonging runs straight and deep
through vulnerability. There's no other way
there." ~ Lisa Purk

Toward the end of each August, a group of my friends from high school get together for an evening. It started a few years ago and I look forward to it every year. One of my best friends from high school is always there as are many we "hung around with." It is an evening of fun, laughter, and reminiscing. "Do you remember? What happened to? Do you ever see?" start many conversations.

And we catch up on life—life as it was back then, life now, and the life we lived in between. For an evening, we get to experience the theme song from *Cheers* as it stirs our emotions with, "where everybody knows your name."

I love these evenings for many reasons. One of them is a sense of connection and belonging. Individuals find this sense of belonging in different ways and in varying places, but we all cherish it.

I have made many mistakes in life in an attempt to garner this sense of belonging. I have stayed in relationships long past their expiration date, tried to be part of groups when I felt like an outsider, and made decisions that I knew weren't in my best interest, telling myself, "It will be alright."

To discover a true sense of connection and belonging, you must be willing to become two things: authentic and vulnerable. These are not two separate things.

It requires a measure of vulnerability to be open to belonging. It also takes being authentic which means you must be—vulnerable. "But what if they don't like me? What if they think I'm nuts? What if they laugh at me?" are all forms of inner chatter that prevent the interplay of vulnerability and authenticity needed in order to gain a fulfilling sense of connection.

The opportunities exist for you to have the sense of connection and belonging you seek, but you can only find them when you're willing to risk being yourself.

Yes, being yourself means there are people who won't necessarily like you. It will mean letting go of groups and people who aren't a good fit for you. But it also means finding the place you truly belong and the satisfaction that brings.

I loved my friends when we were in high school. I think I love them even more now. And each year, I will always return for an evening where everybody knows my name.

And I know theirs.

CHECK IN WITH YOUR INNER CHATTER

1. What fears stop you from finding your sense of belonging and connection? Listen to the inner chatter in your mind to help you identify these. What new thoughts can you use to replace your fear thoughts?

2. Are there places and people you want to release from your circle of connections because you don't have a sense of belonging with them?

3. Who can you engage with where you can be authentic and vulnerable and be accepted as you are?

A DOG NAMED MOLLIE

"Why love, if losing hurts so much? I have no
answers anymore: only the life I have lived.
Twice in that life I've been given the choice: as
a boy and as a man. The boy chose safety, the
man chooses suffering. The pain now is part of
the happiness then. That's the deal."
~ C. S. Lewis in *Shadowlands*

She was a black-and-white beagle named Mollie.
She was also fondly called Moll-Moll; Mollsy; Mollie-girl;
Mollie-Mollie; and Pretty Girl.

Mollie loved people. She loved a good bone, a walk
in the woods (better yet, trust her off her leash and she was
happier—prone to get into trouble, but happy), and a ride
in the car. But mostly, Mollie loved people, especially those
who scratched her ears, back and belly. She wasn't interested
in the other dogs at the dog park. It was their owners who
held the most interest for her.

Mollie's owners were my mom and her husband,
Don. We all loved Mollie. Mom and Don did; my husband
and I did; friends, family, and neighbors did. Even the
neighbor's dogs loved Mollie.

Mollie was with Mom and Don for only a few short
years before she became ill and died unexpectedly. And
so began a process for them—and all of us—of letting go.
Mollie brought great joy to our lives, which is exactly why
losing her brought such pain. Happiness and joy; sadness
and sorrow—the truth is the one only exists and has meaning because of the other.

There are many levels of losing in life that force us
to let go. Some are deeper than others—much deeper. Some

heartbreaks take longer to heal than others. Or as the grief and loss literature tell us, its loss never heals; the burden just becomes easier to bear. Regardless, there is one truth that remains. The pain of letting go exists only because of the joy or comfort we once knew.

I wish I could offer you a way to experience joy and happiness without the risk of experiencing the pain, but I can't. Acknowledge your pain. Remember your joy and walk on holding tight to your memories. Bittersweet as they are, they are an important part of your healing journey.

"The pain now is part of the happiness then. That's the deal." *Shadowlands*—a movie forever etched in my heart for one reason.

It taught me about the deal.

CHECK IN WITH YOUR INNER CHATTER

1. Photos, meaningful objects, and special activities are powerful ways to help you hold tight to your memories. What can you do to erect a memorial to a happy time that has come to an end? Take a trip? Draw a picture? Plant a garden?

2. Have you ever thought that the pain now was part of the happiness then? Does that make sense to you? In what ways does it help you process the pain?

3. Have you been avoiding anything because there may be loss at the end of it? Examples might include a relationship, a dream, or a business. Do you think that's the way God wants you to live?

A VALUES-GUIDED LIFE

"Dear children, let us not love with words or
speech but with action and in truth"
~ 1 John 3:18

I have clients as well as a close personal friend who
have careers as sales directors with Mary Kay. They have explained to me the values they are encouraged to display in
life, which are: God, family, business. Furthermore, they are
encouraged to follow these values in that order—always.

In Mom's final years of life, she experienced frequent
illnesses including hospital and rehab stays. She had increasing care needs even when she was home. During these
times, my husband and I were called on to help her in many
ways and we willingly did so.

When Mom was admitted to the hospital with pneu-
monia, when she was on a ventilator with dangerously low
blood pressure, and when she fell and fractured her pelvis
were all times in my life that my immediate plans changed.

During these and many other times, I needed a way
to make decisions regarding what to do now and what to
delay. I think the values I learned from my Mary Kay connections sum it up well: God first, family second, and business third.

God is first, family second. This means there were
times when my business had to finish in third place. It
meant I had to prioritize within my business and my client care always came first. It also meant I didn't always get
to publish my blog on social media as often as I wanted or
planned.

Was this frustrating and disappointing? Yes, sometimes it was. In order to stay grounded, however, I needed

ways to manage those feelings. One of the most important was to intentionally focus on gratitude. Among other blessings in my life, I was thankful for:

- A mom who never said "I don't have time" when I needed her, even during her busy days in healthcare administration.

- My clients who were flexible and understanding when I needed to change their appointments to a different day and time and who, when I said, "I'm burned out and just need a day to rejuvenate" replied, "It's okay, please take care of yourself."

When life doesn't go as you have it planned, it's important to know your values and let them guide your actions. To help you stay grounded and discover a sense of calm (at least a little bit), you too will benefit from placing your focus on gratitude.

I will always value the ways my husband and I were able to take care of all of our parents. They are bittersweet memories for sure, but I wouldn't trade them for anything.

I only get to hold on to those memories today because of the values that guided my life yesterday.

CHECK IN WITH YOUR INNER CHATTER

1. What values guide your life?

2. What can you do to stay grounded in gratitude when life is messy and filled with unexpected events?

3. How do you make decisions for what activities and tasks you will do now, and which ones will be delayed? or possibly deleted entirely?

DOING WHAT MATTERS TO YOU

"Today you are YOU, that is TRUER than true.
There is NO ONE alive who is YOUER
than YOU!" ~ Dr. Seuss

Have you noticed how each August and September there is a plethora of first day of school pictures posted on social media?

You probably answer that question with a resounding yes. I know this to be true because unless you took a three-week hiatus from Facebook or you don't use social media, you couldn't miss them.

Posting first day of school pictures became a popular trend since the days of social media entered our lives. Scroll your newsfeed and it's not long before you see smiling (or semi-smiling or, in some cases, not-smiling-at-all) children of many ages with signs declaring the grade they're entering this year. There are pictures of children too young for school, but this is their first day with an older brother or sister going back to school. You get it. You've seen it. Maybe you've posted one, too. And that's okay. We've enjoyed seeing them.

I don't have children or grandchildren (nieces, nephews . . . neighbor kids) to share during this back-to-school season.

But if I did, here's what I think would happen:

First, I would forget to buy the supplies and make the obligatory sign.

If I did happen to remember, it would be, relatively speaking, quite lame. It wouldn't be decorated or written in fancy letters because that's just not in my repertoire of skills. My stick figures don't even appear to represent human beings. Please don't ask me about the time I drew one that was, let's just say, clearly male.

But back to the sign . . .

"You could try Pinterest for ideas" you might say, "Uh, that's not likely to happen which has everything to do with 'technology' and 'overwhelmed.'" Enough said.

If the above things happen to come together (i.e., I remember to buy a pretty sign because I know I can't make one myself), then I would forget to take the picture—or I would forget to post it. Or I would get frustrated with the technology of taking the picture and getting it uploaded to whatever social media site I'm posting it to, which I assure you wouldn't be Instagram because well, back to technology. "Next year . . ." I would promise myself.

Or maybe, just maybe, it would all be very Freudian, as in "It just doesn't matter to me" therefore I "forgot." Oops.

Which brings me to my point. Maybe it just simply wouldn't matter to me. Maybe it's not important to you. Then again, maybe it is.

If it's truly important to you and your friends and family are enjoying them, then most definitely keep posting them.

But if you're like me and well, it just isn't, then be okay with that, too.

The point is not whether you posted them. It's being okay if you didn't. It's letting go of guilt and "Well, I should have" if you didn't get it done this year—or any year.

Sometime this year there's going to be something that does matter, and you will share it not because it's a trend, but because *this* (whatever *this* is) truly matters to you. This will be the one you share from the heart of who you are.

I look forward to seeing that picture.

CHECK IN WITH YOUR INNER CHATTER

1. What things are you doing because you think you "should" or because it's a "trend"?

2. What would happen if you chose not to do it?

3. On the flip side, what do you want to do but hesitate because it doesn't seem fashionable?

AN UNEXPECTED EMOTION

"Everybody talks about wanting to change
things and help and fix, but ultimately all you
can do is fix yourself. And that's a lot. Because
if you can fix yourself, it has a ripple effect."
~ Rob Reiner

It was a difficult season in my life.

I was the caregiver for my aging and often ill Mom. This also meant I was witnessing the inevitable and imminent loss of her presence in my life. I didn't know when it would happen, just that it would. Ultimately, she was here longer than I expected, and then suddenly she was gone quicker than I expected.

One day in the midst of it, I was aware of a myriad of emotions. Most of them I could easily understand. "Of course, I feel sad," I told myself. It was the same when I felt scared or confused. I could even understand being stressed, overwhelmed, and frustrated. Sometimes there was even joy and gratitude amidst the uncertain realities. But there was this other one. Why was I feeling "it"?

"It" was anger and all its accompanying expressions. What the heck was that about? I was angry. I felt impatient and ready to lash out. And no one was immune; not even my husband—my sweet, supportive, always-there-for-me husband. I was angry with everyone. I was mad about everything.

Fortunately, for the most part, I didn't lash out. But I was keenly aware of anger's presence.

I recall one morning when I knew it was lurking. It

wasn't particularly welcome as I had enough of it the day before. It was a new day and I wanted to make it a better one.

As I began my quiet time, it was easy to simply seek to release it and replace it with other more peaceful emotions. It would be easy to utter a prayer of, "Please take away this anger." But I also knew that if I did, it would soon show itself again, probably the first time I dropped something, or someone tried to talk to me (Gasp! How dare they?).

And so, instead, I decided to sit with it. I sat calmly in a quiet outdoor space. I connected with myself and my innermost feelings. This time it didn't take long to grasp its meaning. I was angry because I was scared. Dad had already passed several years before. Now I was facing the loss of Mom in my life as well.

Experience tells me it will sometimes take longer to grasp the meaning behind my emotions. I was thankful on this day for grace that offered answers more quickly.

It is understandable for us to want to quickly hide difficult emotions. They're painful and uncomfortable. They're ugly. But our most meaningful, satisfying, and fulfilling lives will only come when we're willing to sit with our emotions—all of them.

Even the angry ones.

CHECK IN WITH YOUR INNER CHATTER

1. What do you do when you are experiencing difficult emotions? Do you try to ignore or release them without digging for what's causing them?

2. Where is a safe space you use to process them? Is it a quiet place of solitude? Or with the help of a trusted confidante?

3. How are your emotions impacting important others around you?

A SMILE
I COULDN'T SEE

"Making one person smile can change the
world. Maybe not the whole world but their
world. Start small. Start now."
~ Unknown author

One morning while out and about for networking
meetings, I decided to get some food at the drive-thru of a
fast food restaurant. Although I tend to avoid these types of
restaurants for a number of reasons, they are readily available and better than choosing the convenience store with its
rows of all things salty and sugary. I was hungry and it would
have taken more than an hour to return home and prepare
a meal. Therefore, the drive-thru won. At least I didn't eat
the greasy potato-like product they call hash browns. But I
digress.

As I ordered my food, I noticed the most pleasant
voice on the speaker. There I was, sitting in line at a fast
food restaurant with no expectations, when suddenly my
attention was captured by a level of friendliness and con-
geniality coming through the speaker. I smiled and felt my
whole body gain an extra measure of relaxation. I thought
about how much her smile impacted me. While I couldn't
see her smile, I could hear it.

The next time you think your verbal demeanor
doesn't matter when someone can't see you, think again.

When you're rushed or distracted, it's reflected in
your voice—and your smile. You will connect more fully
with others when you pay closer attention to your non-verbal
communication. When you consider that communication

is 7% the words you say, 38% your intonation, and 55% your body language, it makes good practice to keep a check on more than the words you choose. Keep a check on what else you're communicating through intonation and body language as well.

I was already having a good day when I stopped by for my meal. However, this woman and her pleasant manner made it even brighter—and I told her so. As we interacted at the next window, I found out her name is Rose. She was the manager, and it was her first day working there. She could have been stressed that day but if she was, she chose instead to share a calm and cheerful manner. She invited me to come back again to her location and I definitely will—for Rose.

I just won't eat the hash browns.

CHECK IN WITH YOUR INNER CHATTER

1. What location do you frequent in a daily but casual way, e.g., a coffee shop on your way to work?

2. Do you know the names of the people at that location? If not, what can you do to learn their names?

3. Make it a point to make a difference in someone's life with a smile or kind word.

A STANLEY CUP WIN

"Whatever affects one directly, affects all
indirectly. I can never be what I ought to be
until you are what you ought to be. This is the
interrelated structure of reality."
~ Dr. Martin Luther King Jr.

I'm a Pittsburgher and have lived there all my life. If you grow up in Pittsburgh, you most likely become a sports fan, especially if one of our teams gets into the post-season. It's what we do. We were at one time referred to as the "City of Champions," and we love our teams.

And so in 2017, with great enthusiasm we followed our beloved Pittsburgh Penguins hockey team battle their way through some tough playoff games. I, along with millions of others, watched, cheered, and held our collective breath. And then one magical night, with uncontained excitement, we watched them hoist the Stanley Cup. Awesome is what we felt. Incredibly awesome.

Then the next morning arrived, the day after the final big win. Was it any different than yesterday? Was my life any better?

Actually, I awakened to find my life was exactly the same as it had been the day before. This wasn't a surprise or a bad thing in any way. Whether or not my favorite team wins or loses, my life remains pretty much the same.

So the morning after, I reflected. What was it about this experience that drew me in to every game, every body check, every penalty, and every point? What kept me coming back game after game? Why was I so drawn to something that had no impact on my life the next morning?

Or did it?

In my time of reflection, here's what I discovered: It does matter for three important reasons:

1. Connection. I experienced the joy of sharing as I watched the games together with both my husband and Mom. We shared pre-game meals together. I watched my then 84-year-old mom begin to learn the game of hockey and learn it with a predictable home-team bias—a memory that still causes me to smile when I picture it. There's such joy in sharing with the people we love, and every playoff series gave us the opportunity to do that.

2. Inspiration. Whether Olympics or professional sports, I am inspired by top-notch athletes who are proficient at their game. Their commitment, discipline, and dedication all speak to me. The emergence of some as leaders and mentors along with their display of teamwork all offer outstanding role models. And their never-give-up effort always amazes me.

3. Fun. Watching the Penguins through the playoff and ultimately to their Stanley Cup win gave me a break, a fun respite from life and business. The playoffs as a focus provided an important diversion I couldn't resist.

So, I had fun and enjoyed a break. As I did, I shared time with my husband and Mom. And it all provided inspiration for my own life when Monday morning rolled around.

Yes, it truly mattered after all.

CHECK IN WITH YOUR INNER CHATTER

1. What is something you believe would bring you joy but you resist because you can't see what difference it would make to your life?

2. Is there another type of value it would bring, e.g., connection with loved ones, inspiration for your goals, or a chance to rest and reignite your energy?

3. What plans can you make today to bring this into your life?

BLESSED SILENCE

"In the attitude of silence, the soul finds the
path in a clearer light, and what is elusive and
deceptive resolves itself into crystal clearness."
~ Tony Scott

Silence.

Upon occasion, I go for what I like to term a "renew-al walk in the woods." These are not the times I hike with my husband or a good friend. These are the times I go alone. Completely alone.

There are many reasons I take quiet walks in the woods. Letting go of some stress is just one of them. It's not unusual, though, to notice resistance in the form of, "I have too much to do; I don't have time for that today; a nap would be just as good;" or "you need to stay in your office and work." This is inner chatter resistance at its best. I can't always explain them, but these thoughts can stand strong between me and the place I know I can renew my mind, my heart—my soul.

In these times, there's only one thing to do: Resist the resistance. I do this by making a choice to put my shoes on and drive to the park. Always a good choice.

Sometimes, I begin the walk with a prayer over a specific situation in my life. At other times, I simply groan, "Help," and trust God knows what I need. And there are the days I don't say a single word. I just start walking.

Then, in blessed silence, I walk. I walk until nature absorbs my stress and my strength and energy return. I walk until nature soaks in my confusion and offers clarity in its place. I walk until my heart is once again filled with hope and my ability to offer gratitude returns.

We all must find ways to push back against resistance. One way is to take the first step toward doing the thing you know will help. One step in that direction leads to two and soon your momentum will shift. But you must take that difficult first step. The second one is easier.

When I resist the resistance and head out for one of my renewal walks in the woods, nature offers what no amount of time in my office or nap ever does.

And then nature says, "Come back again soon."

"I will" I always promise, I will. And I do.

It always starts with resisting the resistance.

CHECK IN WITH YOUR INNER CHATTER

1. What value do you find by intentionally engaging in periods of silence? For example, is silence your way to rest? Cultivate creativity? Release stress?

2. What are your favorite solitude activities?

3. What is one small step you can take to pursue these activities when you find yourself in resistance?

IN THE MIDST
OF MESSINESS

"Count it all joy, my brothers when you meet
trials of various kinds, for you know the testing
of your faith produces steadfastness."
~ James 1:2-3

It was one of our scary and stressful times with Mom's health and her hospital/nursing rehab stays. Layered on that was my being sick for two weeks as I struggled to get past whatever fall season virus invaded my body. Just when we thought my husband had escaped the illness that surrounded him, he got sick. It wasn't a big surprise, but an interruption to our routine nonetheless.

On this occasion, Mom was able to come home from the hospital. On the same day, my cousin and her husband arrived from out of town to stay for a long weekend visit.

I absolutely love spending time with my cousin and her husband and my husband does as well. I always relax and rejuvenate when they're around. I learn and grow and become a better person from our conversations. So, when they asked, "Are you sure it's okay for us to visit; we understand how busy you are right now?" I said without hesitation, "Yes let's stick to our plans; we love spending time with you." And I meant it.

The Monday after they left, I was crazy far behind. My home office had become the "dump zone" for keeping other common areas of our home a little clearer (you know, like have a dining room table where we could actually eat). I had pending e-mails, text messages, and incomplete items on my task list. That didn't count the projects I had been scheduling—and then rescheduling—the necessary time to complete.

But I started that week with a clear mind and a healthy body. I was able to complete tasks and stay focused in a way I wouldn't have the week before. I returned to earlier wake-up times, healthier eating, and getting exercise.

Life is messy sometimes. In the middle of the mess, it can be really tempting to say, "I have to keep going" or "I can't take a break now; I have too much to do." It can seem like the "right thing to do" is to keep pushing through. You might even tell yourself, "It's just the way my life is right now."

Actually, it's just the way you choose it to be.

Don't get me wrong. You didn't choose your stressful life situations as I had not chosen mine. But you do get to choose how you react.

I could have told my cousin this just isn't a good time. They would have understood as would the caring friends who tried to tell me I was taking on too much. But I chose instead to do what we had planned—a weekend of enjoying each other's company. And I did thoroughly enjoy my time with them and after that, I was ready to approach everyday life again.

There are times you need to keep pushing through. But sometimes the thing you most need to do is to stop and enjoy a little time away.

Even in the midst of the messiness.

CHECK IN WITH YOUR INNER CHATTER

1. Do you give yourself permission to take a break when life is busy and stressful?

2. What activities allow you to rest, rejuvenate, and re-energize?

3. Is it time to let yourself engage in some self-care?

BUT I'M OKAY

"I found the secret to life: I'm okay when
everything is not okay." ~ Tori Amos

"How are you? How are you doing? How's it going?
Hey, what's up?"

Consider the different ways this is asked, including
the intonation of the person asking it. This question can
have many different meanings ranging from "Hey, I'm being
friendly and a simple 'I'm good' will do" to "How are you
really? I sincerely want to know."

Through the illnesses and ultimate deaths of our
parents, I had many friends and family asking this question.
Sometimes I really wanted—and needed—to let go and tell
them all of the recent scenarios and especially my myriad of
emotions. Other times, I wanted to say "I'm okay" and then
move on to other topics. I wanted to know what was happening in their lives; I wanted to escape mine for a while. I
wanted to pour into them in the ways they were offering to
pour into me. I wanted to focus on the parts of my life that
weren't causing pain like my business, a book I'm reading,
or my latest baking adventure.

But I'm a person who tries to be strict in my use of
words and so to say, "I'm okay" did not always feel honest. I
was experiencing sadness, fear, and uncertainty. How could
I say, "I'm okay" when my heart wasn't so sure? "They know
what's happening; how can I say I'm okay? What will they
think if I say 'I'm okay'?" These questions anxiously swirled
through my mind in a single moment of time as I heard the
question, "How are you doing?"

Then one day, as I anticipated hearing that question,
I realized, "I *am* okay."

I continue to meet with my clients and lead group workshops . . . I'm okay.

I begin working with new clients . . . I'm okay.

I have coffee with a friend in the morning and dinner with another in the evening . . . I'm okay.

I attend a morning networking event when I'd rather be sleeping or sipping coffee on my patio . . . I'm okay.

I write my blog . . . I'm okay.

I bake; I cook; I do laundry . . . I'm okay.

And sometimes, I take a break from it all and I sleep, or sip that coffee, or stare at mindless TV. I'm okay.

Saying "I'm okay" in reply to "How are you doing" doesn't mean you don't feel sadness, fear, anxiety, or other painful emotions. It simply means that in the midst of it all, you continue with life. Maybe you're not doing it as well as you would do in less stressful times. But you're doing it. You're not hiding or giving up on all other things in life. You put one foot in front of the other and keep going. Maybe you don't do everything; but you do something. Maybe you don't do it with the joy or spark you typically would, but you do it anyway.

So, the next time someone asks, "How are you?" and you want to talk about anything except what's painful in your life, choose to say, "I'm okay."

Because you are . . . and I am, too.

CHECK IN WITH YOUR INNER CHATTER

1. Who are your best people to talk with when something sad and painful is happening in your life? Are you turning to them to help you process your emotions?

2. Make a list of the ways you are continuing on with life despite your sadness.

3. Create a mantra of, "I'm okay" or similar wording to repeat to yourself throughout your day. The more you say, "I'm okay," the more you will be even as the sorrow lingers.

LET IT BE

"Be still and know that I am God."
~ Psalm 46:10

It wasn't the first time.

I noticed my thoughts were consumed with what could be termed, "Trying to figure it all out." I could sum up those thought wanderings with this one question: "What is going to happen . . . and when?"

You might recognize these kinds of thoughts. They sound something like, "Well, maybe 'this' is going to happen; I think 'that' will happen; Or I hope or I wish that . . ." It might even start with, "I want . . ." There are many variations to these types of thoughts. They can be intrusive and at times you might find yourself, as I did, ruminating on them. But they all boil down to this: We want to know what is going to happen in the future. We can be especially prone to this kind of thinking when circumstances are creating fear and uncertainty because those circumstances are beyond our control.

One day, as I struggled to release the hold these thoughts had on me, I became aware of new words coming into my space. I smiled as my awareness fell upon, "Let it be" as the thought calmly and softly drifted into my mind, my heart, and my spirit. It was a clear message from God; "Let it be, I've got this. Trust Me."

Since that day, each time I notice my thoughts swirling around "What is going to happen? Will it be 'this' or 'that?'", I stop and remind myself to "let it be." I whisper a word of gratitude that I am not alone.

It brings me back to the present. It grounds me. I find a place of peace and I renew my strength for the moment. It reminds me that I can trust God for my future—whatever my future holds.

And, I let it be.

CHECK IN WITH YOUR INNER CHATTER

1. When a worry or fear-filled thought about the future enters your mind, ask yourself, "Do I have everything I need for today?" Then affirm your trust in God for tomorrow.

2. If your thought is one of, "I should have done more for <insert person/situation>, gain wisdom by asking yourself, "What did I learn" and "What can I do differently in the future?"

3. Are you comparing yesterday's performance with today's knowledge? Remind yourself, "I did the best I could do at the time I was doing it; now that I know better, I'll do better."

VALUING CORE NEEDS

"I need some space away from you so I can love
myself more and so that I can love you even
better." ~ Unknown author

The word *need* is a tricky word.

Anyone who knows me well knows I encourage being purposeful in the use of this word. I do so for myself,
and that same encouragement extends to my clients. I will
highlight it for close friends if I think it is inhibiting them
in some way. I do so because the word is oftentimes used as
a default. As such, it creates stress while lacking intention.
Consider times that you have said, "I know I need to . . ,"
often without the follow through of action steps.

Conversely, understanding your core needs has
great value.

When I experience feelings of impatience, even anger, and the reason is not readily apparent to me, I intentionally seek to understand the cause. When I did so on one
specific occasion, an answer became clear to me: My need
for solitude was not being fulfilled. I was not taking care of
my personal need for quiet and alone time that calms and
revitalizes me.

We all have needs that are important to us. Without
fulfilling them, we can become angry and impatient.
Other results might include fatigue and lack of concentration; we might find ourselves overeating, overspending, or
over-scheduling. Or possibly, we'll notice all of the above.

Another sign that your needs are not being fulfilled
are knee-jerk reactions to old thought patterns you believed
were conquered but are suddenly challenging for you again.

When your needs are not being met, the things you won't find are energy, satisfaction, or fulfillment. Happiness, joy, and gratitude will remain elusive.

Gaining clarity around your personal needs is highly beneficial for daily routines as well as times when life circumstances challenge you emotionally. You can only honor your needs when you know what they are. Others can only be supportive of your needs when they know what they are.

Have you identified what your core needs are? Have you communicated these to the important people around you who can support you in them?

When I hear myself repeatedly saying, "I know I need to . . .," but have no follow through, I have two options. I can drown in the stress and frustration of it, or I can intentionally set action steps and stick to the plan.

But when I find myself unnecessarily angry and impatient, then it's time to ask, "Do I have a need that's not being fulfilled?" Chances are, spending some time alone will do the trick.

It's usually all I need.

CHECK IN WITH YOUR INNER CHATTER

1. Identify three of your core needs. These are the things that when absent, you are not your best for yourself or your loved ones around you.

2. What do you notice about yourself when these needs are not being fulfilled?

3. What actions can you take to be sure you're fulfilling your needs on a regular basis?

WALKING WITH GOD

"I will walk by faith even when I cannot see."
~ 2 Corinthians 5:7

Life had caught up with me. Cough and extreme fatigue were lingering from a recent virus. A bout of cystitis arrived despite the "very unwelcome" status I place on it. The gray and dreary cold of a Western Pennsylvania winter had me craving yet-to-be-available sunshine. The pain of missing Mom was particularly sharp.

And so, a weekend of do-nothingness was exactly what I wanted. I finished a really enjoyable book and started a new one. I slept. I slept more. My husband and I watched the Olympics together. We watched events we had already watched. I slept more. I slept so many hours over that weekend, I thought I wouldn't be able to sleep Sunday night—but I did.

In the midst of it, I attended a Valentines Tea I had been invited to and it too was exactly what I needed. Surrounded by a group of loving and supportive women who shared kind words and supportive hugs, I walked away affirmed that my do-nothingness was not only acceptable, but good for me. I needed that, too. Receiving affirmation that my do-nothingness was okay helped me to be open to engaging in doing just that—nothing.

Waking up Monday morning wasn't easy. When the alarm rang, I was still sleeping soundly. But my day was scheduled, and it didn't include what the weekend had held. Nor was I inclined to reschedule any part of it.

My first thought was how much I wanted to stay in bed. My next thought was how much I didn't. My transition thought was a prayer and a realization.

I trust God to be there for me. Relying on Him in increasing ways is part of my life focus. On that particular morning, I needed Him to walk with me. But He can only walk with me if I have chosen to take steps and be in motion. And so, I offered a prayer asking both for His help while also thanking Him in belief that He would indeed be with me through the day. Then I put my feet on the floor, and I walked.

I believe God's love for us is there whether we're in bed feeling sad and tired or productively going about our days. But if we want Him to walk with us throughout our days, then we must put ourselves in motion. The action we're taking must be aligned with the prayer we're praying.

For me, it was a do-nothing weekend that became a Monday of progress that began with trust.

I walked.

God came along with me.

CHECK IN WITH YOUR INNER CHATTER

1. What are your habits when you're feeling sadness in life? Are they healthy or unhealthy?

2. Do you give yourself permission for rest when you are experiencing a difficult loss in your life?

3. What can you do to rely on God to help you through difficult times?

PEACE IN THE MIDST OF IT

"Life with God is not immunity from
difficulties, but peace in difficulties."
~ C.S. Lewis

My husband and I had tickets to see the comedian,
Michael Jr., at a local church. We'd had the tickets for a few
weeks but one of Mom's unexpected illnesses and hospital
stays caused us to question if we should go or not. It was a
difficult decision.

In the end, we decided to go. We visited with Mom
and stayed until the last possible moment. Our dinner was
take-out from a Wendy's drive-thru that we ate while we
sat in the car rather than the nice dinner out at a favorite
restaurant as we had planned. In case of an emergency, I
had my phone sitting squarely in my lap and set on vibrate.

For a few hours, we got to laugh and feel joy in the
moment. Our minds got to escape to a happier place for a
while.

When life circumstances are challenging, it can be
easy to get lost in the sorrow. But our experience with going
to the show reminded me that in the midst of sadness, fear,
and uncertainty, there is still the opportunity for gratitude,
peace, and joy.

When my grandfather died in 1978, I was a senior
in high school. I remember sitting in my grandmother's
kitchen with Mom, my aunt, and Grandma. I don't recall
what was said but the four of us began to laugh about something; and then I was quickly struck with a pang of guilt as
I thought, "How can we be laughing? Grandpap just died."

Mom assured me it was okay that we were laughing together, that it didn't mean we didn't care about Grandpap. It was one of my first lessons that there can be joy even amidst the sorrow.

I encourage you to find ways to unlock your own peace and joy and let them be your companions as you journey through sadness and uncertainty. One of mine is my morning quiet time in which I connect with my own thoughts and emotions and, most importantly, with God.

"The peace of God which surpasses all understanding" (Philippians 4:7) has become real for me. I sincerely don't understand the peace I feel at times. And yet, it is there. Even amid the sadness, fear and uncertainty, there is the peace.

What would I do without it?

I simply don't know.

CHECK IN WITH YOUR INNER CHATTER

1. Do you allow yourself time and space to feel peace, even a moment of joy, when your life is full to the brim with sad and painful events?

2. What habits can you establish to cultivate your connection to God's peace?

3. It is often said that "laughter is the best medicine." What can you do that engages you in fits of laughter?

TRASH OR TREASURE?

"For where your treasure is there will your
heart be also." ~ Luke 12:34

My husband and I enjoy spending a few hours on
Saturday mornings exploring local yard sales. Some summers we score several items as we enjoy sunny weekend
mornings together. One of his favorites is a picture now
hanging in our family room. One of my favorites is a ce-
ramic water jug that matches the theme of my office. Or is it
the Victorian Santa? It's difficult for me to choose.

Regardless of which is our favorite item, there is one
thing we say every time we go exploring: One person's trash
is another one's treasure.

This reminds me of the power of word choices.

I don't choose (and I encourage my clients to avoid)
the word *selfish*. It has negative connotations and I believe
prevents someone from engaging in healthy self-care activities because their minds quietly scream *selfish* and their gut
responds with a knot of guilt. My health coach friend is per-
fectly fine using the word as she defines it as "it's okay to be
selfish when it comes to taking care of oneself."

A business consultant friend and I were recently
leading a discussion on collaboration and the word *failure*
came into the conversation. This is another word I choose to
avoid, and I reframe it as "What did I learn?" or "How did I
grow from the experience?" My friend absolutely embraces
the word *failure* and believes it's important to be comfortable with using the word. It's interesting that our end result
is the same: to look at what worked, what didn't, and what
we learned. I resist the word *failure*; she openly says, "That
failed . . . now what?"

I am particular about word choices and encourage my clients to be so as well. And so, I found these conversations quite interesting. I have always been able to see both sides of most issues. It was no different with these word choice conversations. I embraced my view but easily understood their points as well.

All of which leads me back to yard sales and *trash* versus *treasure*.

To be selfish or not to be selfish, to fail or not fail— those are not the issues.

The issue or question is, "Is your word choice defeating you?" If so, then it's trash. Or "Is your word choice empowering you, moving you forward, and supporting you in becoming better today than you were yesterday?" If that's the case, then it's your treasure.

Are the words you're choosing, *trash* or *treasure*?

CHECK IN WITH YOUR INNER CHATTER

1. As you observe your choice of words, notice the associated feeling you experience. If it reflects fear, worry, or self-doubt, choose instead to find new words that empower you.

2. What do you notice when there is misalignment between your words and what's in your heart?

3. Do you experience stress and self-doubt when your thoughts are different from someone else's thoughts?

THE THINGS WE PACK

"Argue for your limitations, and sure enough,
they're yours." ~ Richard Bach

I like to travel. Sometimes it's going to places I've been before and rediscovering the things I enjoyed the first time I was there. I like the familiarity of it. Other times, it's the adventure of going somewhere I've never been and discovering new places and things to do. Either way, there are two things I must do: pack and unpack.

I don't enjoy either of these activities all that much. Making several days' worth of "What do I want to wear" decisions taxes me. And I am an over-packer. Every time. But at least when I'm packing, I'm looking forward to time away.

Unpacking is easier because there are no decisions to make. But I'm home, my vacation is over, and my everyday routine is looming. And there are all these pieces of stuff that need to be put away. I admit it can take me days (weeks even).

As I am continually on the look-out for how everyday experiences teach us something about life, so it is with packing and unpacking. It speaks to me of thoughts.

Life is often compared to a journey and our thoughts are something we must take along with us. It's non-negotiable. And just like choosing what to take on my trips, we get to choose what thoughts we take on our journey around life.

If I take my favorite summer dress on a trip where I'll be biking and hiking, that doesn't serve me very well. It makes much more sense for me to pack my favorite hiking boots, cargo pants, and options that account for variations in weather and provide what's needed to fully enjoy my vacation or weekend escape.

It's the same with our thoughts. When we habitual-
ly carry thoughts of not being "enough" in some way, e.g.,
smart enough, young enough, or disciplined enough, we are
not serving ourselves well. Other defeating thought patterns
that might ring through our minds are, "It's not meant for
me; If only I had the time (money; support . . .) or I don't
have the right education." The variety of negative thoughts
is vast. All of them will hold us back from pursuing our
most fulfilling life, whether it's a new adventure, education,
opening a business, or writing a book.

Alternatively, when you cultivate a habit of believing
you already have—or are intelligent enough to gain—the
skills, talents, and resources you need, then you'll pursue
what offers you the most satisfying life. It takes being intentional and it doesn't happen overnight. If you want to pack a
more positive thought habit, you can begin with what you're
injecting into your mind through what you read and watch
and the company you keep.

Travel involves packing and unpacking that which
will serve you well for your trip. When you view your life
this same way, you'll be intentional in unpacking what isn't
working. You'll pack what does.

Even if you over pack, you'll be sure to have what
you need for your journey.

CHECK IN WITH YOUR INNER CHATTER

1. Observe your thoughts and ask, "Are these thoughts helping me or hindering me?"

2. What parts of your life are in a holding pattern because of
   defeating thoughts?

3. What new thoughts would help you take forward-mov-
   ing action steps?

ABOUT LISA PURK

Lisa Purk started Lisa Purk Life Coaching LLC because she wanted to help others learn how to harness the power of their own thoughts.

As a middle-aged woman, Lisa recognized her own unhappiness and lack of fulfillment and started a journey of self-discovery. She realized that if she wanted to change her life and relationships, she had to change her own inner chatter. She now helps others do the same through individual and group coaching, writing, and leading workshops.

Lisa lives near Pittsburgh, PA with her husband, Rick, and spends her free time reading, doing puzzles, and hiking or biking the trails of Ohiopyle, PA. To learn more about Lisa, go to www.lisapurklifecoaching.com.

KEEP IN TOUCH WITH LISA PURK

Would you like to learn more about how to release your own defeating inner chatter?

To receive your copy of Lisa's free e-book, *4 Steps to Releasing Your Defeating Inner Chatter* or to request a complimentary consultation with her, go to:
www.lisapurklifecoaching.com
and complete the "Get in Touch" form.

Lisa loves hearing from her readers! While you're there, you can also sign-up to receive Lisa's weekly newsletter, *Inner Chatter Matters*, by following the link at the bottom of the home page.

What experiences did you have from applying the lessons learned from this book? Did you discover how to see your everyday experiences from a different perspective?

Please e-mail Lisa at lisa@lisapurklifecoaching.com to share your stories with her.

Follow Lisa on Facebook at **Lisa Purk Life Coaching** and request to join her private group, **Purk Up Your Life**, for more daily inspiration and insights.